W9-COV-209

LEWIS HAYDEN

and the

WAR AGAINST SLAVERY

Lewis Hayden, around 1858
By permission of the Houghton Library, Harvard University

LEWIS HAYDEN

and the

WAR AGAINST SLAVERY

by

JOEL STRANGIS

LINNET BOOKS

1999

This work was prepared with the assistance of a research grant from the Society of Children's Book Writers and Illustrators.

First published in 1999 as a Linnet Book,
an imprint of The Shoe String Press, Inc.,
2 Linsley Street, North Haven, Connecticut 06473.

Library of Congress Cataloging-in-Publication Data
Strangis, Joel.
    Lewis Hayden and the war against slavery / by Joel Strangis.
      p. cm.
    Includes index.
    Summary: A biography of a former slave who was active in the anti-slavery movement, as a fugitive in Canada, a "stationmaster" on the Underground Railroad, a supporter of John Brown, and a recruiter for "black regiments."
      ISBN 0-208-02430-1 (cloth: alk. paper).
      1. Hayden, Lewis, c.1811–1889—Juvenile literature.   2. Afro-American abolitionists—Biography—Juvenile literature.   3. Abolitionists—United States—Biography—Juvenile literature.   4. Antislavery movements—United States—History—19th century—Juvenile literature.
    [1. Hayden, Lewis, c.1811–1889.   2. Abolitionists.   3. Afro-Americans—Biography.   4. Antislavery movements.]   I. Title.
E449.H39S77   1998   98-29406
973.7'114'092—dc21   CIP
[B]   AC

Designed by Jennie Malcolm
Printed in the United States of America

For my mother and father

CONTENTS

The law will never make men free; it is men who have got to make the law free. They are the lovers of law and order who observe the law when the government breaks it.

Henry David Thoreau
"Slavery in Massachusetts"
1854

AUTHOR'S NOTE

I have struggled with the terms to describe the race of characters in this work. The term "African-American" is out of place in the pre-Civil War era when few citizens of the United States thought of themselves as "Americans." In general, during this period "African" was used either as a derogatory term or to describe a person actually born in Africa. The terms "Negro" (sometimes "negro") and "colored" appear only when quoting the exact words of a participant.

When appropriate, I have described characters as "black" or "white." "Black" refers to persons of African descent and "white" refers to persons of European descent. Readers should keep in mind that not all blacks were slaves—many anti-slavery leaders of African descent, including John Mifflin Brown, Robert Morris and Charles Lenox Remond, were never slaves. Nor were all slaves dark-skinned. As you will read, Ellen Craft's skin was so light she was able to escape from slavery disguised as a slave owner.

When possible, I have tried to allow the characters to tell their own stories. In quotations I have retained the original spellings. Where a misspelling might be blamed on the author (or the editor), I have indicated that I am following the original with the term "[*sic*]," meaning "thus."

Source notes are necessary for scholars and helpful for students, but the small numbers perched above the text can be a distraction for casual readers. I have tried to meet the needs of all parties by using enough notes to allow scholars to check facts and students to get more information, without unnecessary interruption. When undocumented quotations appear, readers can assume that the next note (which may not occur for one or more paragraphs) will give the reference for that quotation as well.

In some chapters I have used dialogue to illustrate the action as well as the intentions of the characters. The scenes I have created (such as Lewis Hayden's meeting with John Brown) are indicated by a change in type style. All persons named in them are real and all events described by the characters themselves are historically accurate.

INTRODUCTION

You are about to read the story of a criminal. Lewis Hayden was a fugitive from Kentucky; he was arrested twice in Massachusetts; and he participated in a conspiracy that resulted in the execution of seven men in Virginia. He also conducted operations in New York, Ohio, Michigan, Pennsylvania, and Canada.

Hayden's crimes included theft of valuable property, riotous behavior, and plotting against the government. His crimes also included helping slaves escape to freedom, feeding the hungry, sheltering the homeless, and holding an unquenchable belief in the equality of all persons whether white or black, male or female.

Perhaps more than any other American, Hayden experienced the full range of the anti-slavery struggle. He was a fugitive slave and he was a stationmaster on the Underground Railroad. He traveled from town to town speaking against slavery and he took up arms against slavery. He recruited soldiers for black regiments and he suffered the loss of a son who had enlisted in the Navy. He was a co-worker with Wendell Phillips, William Lloyd Garrison, Theodore Parker, Harriet Beecher Stowe, and a host of lesser known campaigners.

Despite his accomplishments and his famous allies, Hayden is not well known. Perhaps this is so because he was not a writer like Garrison, or Stowe, or William Wells Brown. Nor was he an orator like Phillips, or Parker, or Frederick Douglass. As writers and orators these individuals fought for freedom with powerful words. Their publications and their speeches brought attention to themselves and left a record for future generations.

Hayden and many of his friends were committed to freedom through action. In the language of our times, they were "activists." We know relatively little about these activists because many of their deeds were illegal by the standards of their day. Hayden's assistance to fugitive slaves, his militant defense of William and Ellen Craft, his rescue of the escaped slave Shadrach, and his role in John Brown's conspiracy were illegal at the time, no matter how commendable they may seem to us today.

Hayden and his friends could not reveal the specifics of their activities during the dangerous period from 1840 to the Civil War. If we are missing the exact route of a trip through the Underground Railroad, or the details of John Brown's visits to Boston, it is very likely because the participants made a conscious effort to hide that information.

Near the end of the nineteenth century, a few of the anti-slavery activists recorded their experiences. A few others had children to record their deeds. Hayden had no surviving children and did not preserve a record of his actions.

For these reasons, Hayden has never received the credit he is due. His story is told only in footnotes of the biographies of the leading men and women of the anti-slavery movement. Using the thread of Hayden's remaining letters and the newspaper reports of his day, I have tried to sew those footnotes together in order to tell the remarkable story of a man committed to the fight for human rights.

PROLOGUE:
A MOTHER AND CHILD

I belonged to the Rev. Adam Rankin, a Presbyterian minister in Lexington, Kentucky.

My mother was of mixed blood—white and Indian. She married my father when he was working in a bagging factory near by. After a while my father's owner moved off and took my father with him, which broke up the marriage. She was a very handsome woman. My master kept a large dairy, and she was the milk-woman. Lexington was a small town in those days, and the dairy was in the town. Back of the college was the Masonic lodge. A man who belonged to the lodge saw my mother when she was about her work. He made proposals of a base nature to her. When she would have nothing to say to him, he told her she need not be so independent, for if money could buy her, he would have her. My mother told old mistress, and begged that master might not sell her. But he did sell her. My mother had a high spirit, being part Indian. She would not consent to live with this man, as he wished; and he sent her to prison, and had her flogged, and punished in various ways, so that at last she began to have crazy turns. . . . She tried to kill herself several times once with a knife and once by hanging. She had long, straight black hair, but after this it all turned white, like an old person's. When she had raving turns, she always talked about her children. The jailer told the owner that if he would let her go to her children, perhaps she would get quiet. They let her out one time, and she came to the place where we were. I might have been seven or eight years old,—don't know my age exactly. I was not at home when she came. I came in and found her in one of the cabins near the kitchen. She sprung and caught my arms, and seemed going to break them, and then said, "I'll fix *you* so they'll never get you!" I screamed, for I thought she was going to kill me; they came in and took me away. They tied her, and carried her off.

Lewis Hayden to Harriet Beecher Stowe (1853).[1]

1. A Slave in Lexington

Lewis Hayden did not know how old he was when he was attacked by his mother. Hayden could not be sure of his age since the birth dates of slaves were rarely recorded. Slaves were not considered important enough to have birth records or even birthdays. The best indications are, however, that Lewis Hayden, the son of Millie and Lewis Hayden, was born in Lexington, Kentucky about 1811.

By law, young Lewis was automatically the property of his mother's owner, Adam Rankin, even though his father was owned by another man. In addition to Lewis and his mother, Reverend Rankin owned other slaves (some of whom were Lewis's brothers and sisters), the dairy operation where Millie worked, and a substantial house.

Years later, looking back on his childhood, Lewis realized the irony of his mother's sale away from her children by a Christian minister. Even as an adult he painfully recalled Rankin's cruelty:

> I never saw anything in Kentucky which made me sup-
> pose that ministers or professors of religion considered

it any more wrong to separate the families of slaves by sale than to separate any domestic animals.

There may be ministers and professors of religion who think it is wrong, but I never met with them. My master was a minister, and yet sold my mother . . ."[1]

As Lewis Hayden learned, mothers could be separated from their children because slaves lived in a system that treated human beings as property. Slaves could be bought, sold, rented, or given as gifts. In addition, owners were free to punish their slaves as they saw fit, since the slave system assumed owners would not unnecessarily harm their valuable "property."

This assumption was frequently wrong. After Rankin sold Millie Hayden, she was whipped and tortured to the point of insanity because she refused to have sex with her new master. Other slaveowners punished disobedient slaves by cropping an ear or cutting off a toe. Starvation, heated pokers, and broken bones were also used for obtaining obedience. The ultimate punishment for most slaves, however, was to be sold away from their families, as Millie was sold away from her children.

But slaves were separated from their families for many reasons, not just as punishment. If a slaveowner died without a will, his slaves were often auctioned off as a convenient way to divide the estate. Slaveowners short of cash could be forced by creditors to sell slaves in order to pay off debts. Or a slaveowner might decide to "put a slave in his pocket" by selling the slave and pocketing the cash as Rankin did with Millie Hayden.

One of Lewis Hayden's most memorable experiences as a slave occurred when he was about fourteen years old and still the property of Adam Rankin. In May 1825, the French hero of the

American Revolution, the Marquis de Lafayette, visited Lexington and the county, Fayette, that bore his name.

On that spring morning, Lewis escaped from his chores and ran to the edge of town to watch Lafayette's arrival. Lewis knew a slave boy would not be welcome among the festively dressed adults. He moved away from the crowd and found a solitary spot on top of a split-rail fence where he could watch the parade.

The parade began with local heroes. The first unit, a cavalry division, came over the hill with sabers rattling and brass shining. Veterans of the American Revolution followed in the next group. The horsemen probably waved and tipped their hats to the cheering crowd, but they would have paid little attention to a slave boy watching from atop the fence.

As the riders passed in front of him, Lewis could see Lafayette's open carriage approaching. Following the lavishly decorated carriage were more soldiers on horseback, then town dignitaries, followed by professors and students from the local university.

When Lafayette's carriage reached Lewis, the Marquis bowed graciously in the youngster's direction. Lewis looked around. He was still alone. The great man had bowed down to him, a slave! Lewis was so surprised he fell off the fence. Jumping up, he ran after Lafayette thinking to himself, "Come foot, help body," and he followed the Marquis's carriage all the way into town.[2]

Walking back to Rankin's house afterwards, Lewis thought about his experience. His brief encounter with Lafayette had taught him that one group of people had no right to hold another group in chains. Hayden later told friends, "Lafayette was the most famous man I had ever heard of, and you can imagine how I felt, a slave-boy to be favored with his recognition. That act burnt his image upon my heart so that I shall never need a permit to recall it. I date my hatred of slavery from that day."[3]

A few months after Lafayette's visit, Adam Rankin decided to return to his native Pennsylvania. In the winter of 1826, Rankin sold his Lexington home and made his final preparations. Since he could not take his slaves into Pennsylvania, a free state, he chose to sell them at public auction.

On a cold February morning, Lewis Hayden, his brothers, and his sisters were led to the auction to be sold with Rankin's furniture, livestock, and other slaves.

The sale probably started with furniture. In those days handsome chairs sold for $5 to $10. A china set was worth $25. An attractive clock might have gone for $33. Livestock would have been paraded before the crowd. A cow and calf could be bought for $45. A good horse might bring $80.

Customarily, after the household goods were sold and the livestock auctioned to the highest bidder, the slaves were led to the auction block. Despite the freezing February weather, the auctioneer would not have hesitated to strip a young man in order to show his muscles. A strong young man could bring $600. A small boy, still not able to walk, might be sold for $80—then torn from his mother's arms and delivered to his new owner. Spectators often heard the cries of husbands and wives as new masters led them in opposite directions.

As Lewis Hayden waited his turn, he could see the hated slave traders at the back of the crowd. Older slaves probably warned him about the traders. "If they get you, you're 'sold down the river,'" was the warning. "They'll take you south, to Memphis or New Orleans. Sell you at auction to some big rice swamp or to a cotton plantation. In that swamp or on that plantation, they'll work you to death. You'll go in, but you'll never come out."

Watching the bidders compete for his brothers and sisters, Lewis had a feeling he would not be sold on the block. He thought

Lewis Hayden was traded for a carriage and a pair of horses when he was fifteen. This ad of February 9, 1826 may have initiated that trade. Courtesy of the Lexington Public Library

Rankin might take him into Pennsylvania. Once in a free state, Lewis planned to escape and get free.

Lewis's notion that he would not be sold at auction was partly correct. When his turn came to climb the auction block, an assistant to the auctioneer pulled him aside. He would not be sold on the block, but he was not going to Pennsylvania either. Rankin had traded him to a man named Warner for a carriage and a pair of matched horses.

Lewis was stunned. In one moment, his emotions had taken him from slave to free man and back to slave. As Rankin and Warner worked out the details of the sale, Lewis examined the carriage and horses. A few months before he had been the equal of a marquis. Now he was the equal of a carriage and two horses. The young slave looked at the horses and mumbled bitterly, "For *them* I have been sold!"[4]

Hayden's new master was Elijah Warner, a manufacturer and peddler of clocks and cabinets. Warner made a fortune trading his manufactured goods for feathers, quilts, homemade jeans, and other nonperishable items available from backwoods settlers.

As Warner's slave, Hayden accompanied his master on his trips through Kentucky. Hayden's duties probably included loading and unloading trade goods, caring for the horses, and occasionally driving the wagon.

Despite his bondage, Hayden profited from his experiences with Warner. In the country inns where they stayed, Hayden probably ate out-of-doors or in the kitchen with other slaves. After dinner, however, he could slip into the dining room to clear his master's plate or to fill his pipe, and then crouch in a corner listening as Warner discussed the issues of the day with other guests. From his travels and the discussions he heard, Hayden received an education in geography, politics, and human nature denied to all but a few slaves.

When Elijah Warner died in the fall of 1829, he was one of the wealthiest men in Lexington. His estate was valued in excess of $85,000. The list of customers owing him money went on for forty-four pages and included accounts in thirty-four Kentucky counties. In his will, Warner left his son, William, $22,000, including a home and seven slaves. Warner bequeathed his daughter, Elmira, $33,000, including a home and nine slaves, one of them being a "Negro boy named Lewis at the valuation of $325."

Lewis Hayden remained the property of the Warner family throughout the 1830s. During this period he was allowed to marry Esther Harvey, a slave owned by a Lexington merchant, Joseph Harvey. While Lewis and Esther considered themselves married, slaveowners only recognized their relationship as a union of convenience. If slaveowners allowed a wedding ceremony, they often used the phrase "till death *or distance* do you part." In other words, the couple were married *until* the owner decided to sell one or the other to a new owner who did not live in the area.

As with many slave couples, Esther and Lewis also had to overcome the barrier of being owned by separate masters. Whether the slave husband and the slave wife lived together, or whether they even got to see one another, was entirely a decision of their owners.

Lewis and Esther had a son who was added to Harvey's property. When Harvey's business failed, his slaves and his other property were sold at auction to pay his creditors. Esther and her child were purchased by Henry Clay.

Clay was a successful Lexington lawyer and the most important politician in Kentucky. By the time he acquired Esther in about 1836, Clay had been a member of the United States Senate, Speaker of the House of Representatives, and Secretary of State under President John Quincy Adams.

Although Clay owned slaves, he was considered a moderate on the slavery issue. He believed the federal government had no right to restrict slavery within the states, but he favored a policy of slowly freeing the slaves called "gradual emancipation." Clay was president of the American Colonization Society, which raised money to send freed slaves to colonies in Africa.

Unfortunately, Lewis and Esther Hayden did not see Henry Clay as the generous advocate of gradual emancipation. While Clay's slave, Esther gave birth to a second child, but the baby died soon thereafter. About a month after this, Esther ran crying to her husband. Clay had sold her and their surviving son to one of the hated slave traders. Hayden was powerless to stop the sale and could only watch as his wife and child were dragged away, never to be seen again.

When Hayden asked Clay for a reason for selling Esther and the boy, Clay replied haughtily that "he had bought them and had sold them."[5] Hayden was devastated. Slaves sales had separated him from his mother, his brothers and sisters, and now from his wife and child. Years later he wrote, "I have one child who is buried in Kentucky and that grave is pleasant to think of. I've got another that is sold nobody knows where, and that I can never bear to think of."[6]

As property of the Warner family, Hayden performed a variety of tasks, tasting almost every level of slave life. For a while he was assigned to work in one of Lexington's bagging factories. In these hot and dusty buildings, slaves turned Lexington's principal cash crop, hemp, into bagging for Southern cotton and rope for sailing ships. Although Lewis survived the experience with no ill effects, he must have seen other slaves worked to death, unable to breathe from the airborne fibers that often caused a fatal, pneumonia-like disease.

Hayden soon met and married Harriet Bell, the slave of Patterson Bain. When they married, Harriet already had a two-year-old son, Joseph, whom Lewis treated as his own. Not long thereafter, Lewis was approached by some friends about escaping and "heading for the North Star." Hayden refused. He knew that going north to a free state would require many nights of running through woods and fields; hiding and resting by day. Harriet and Joseph could never make it. As much as he wanted to be free, Hayden refused to go without his wife and son.

In 1840 the Warners sold Hayden to a cruel master who frequently whipped him and demanded long days of hard labor. Hayden made good use of these days, however, by learning to read, as he studied the Bible and discarded newspapers.[7] Two years later, Hayden was

FOR SALE,

A LIKELY NEGRO MAN 24 years of age, a first rate bagging weaver and farm hand, any one wishing to purchase such a negro will apply to the subscriber.

WM. A. WARNER.

Lexington, jan 4, 1840. 71-4w.
(Intelligencer copy 4 weeks.)

The "Likely Negro Man" advertised in 1840 for sale by William Warner, the son of Elijah Warner, could have been Hayden. Courtesy of the Lexington Public Library

sold again and he became the property of a partnership consisting of Lewis Baxter and Thomas Grant. Baxter and Grant ignored Lewis's family name and referred to their new slave as "Lewis Grant."

Calling slaves by the name of the owner was an accepted custom in the slave states. Although his name had always been "Lewis Hayden," as the young slave moved through a succession of owners he was referred to as "Lewis Rankin," then as "Lewis Warner," and—when Elmira Warner married Thomas Van Sweringen—as "Van Sweringen's Lewis." Stripping a slave of a family name denied the importance of families in the slave community and made it easier to separate a slave from his or her family when the time came.

Hayden's new owners apparently were not wealthy men. Baxter was a clerk in an insurance office. Grant was a dealer in lanterns, candles, and lantern oil. They did not purchase Hayden for their own use, but rather as an investment to be leased to others.

By the summer of 1844, Baxter and Grant had leased their slave

The Phoenix Hotel on Main Street, where Hayden was a waiter, was Lexington's main gathering spot for the well-to-do. Courtesy of Archives and Special Collections, University of Kentucky Libraries

to John Brennan, owner of the Phoenix Hotel, Lexington's foremost establishment for eating and lodging. Brennan's contract for Lewis's services extended through the end of the fall horse races, Lexington's busiest season for visitors.

Leasing a slave was such a common practice that standard conditions existed. In addition to his cash payment to Baxter and Grant, Brennan would have been responsible for housing and feeding Hayden. According to the traditional written agreement, Brennan would have also promised to provide the slave with a "sufficient supply of good and reasonable clothing"; and if Hayden became sick, Brennan would have to take "care of him and pay the doctor bill."[8]

Brennan assigned Hayden to work as a waiter in the dining room. Hayden's intelligence and the knowledge he had gained from his travels must have been significant assets as he waited on Lexington's prominent visitors. Hayden was successful enough as a waiter to accumulate some cash savings, possibly from tips and from running errands after hours.

As the summer came to a close, Lewis Hayden had good reasons to worry about himself and his family. The contract for his services to Brennan would expire on September 30, the end of the racing season. Would Baxter and Grant reassign Hayden or would they "sell him down the river," never to see Harriet and Joseph again? Now that Joseph was about seven years old, how much longer would he be allowed to live with his mother? When would Bain decide to put Joseph in his pocket by selling him for cash?

Lewis Hayden decided it was time for his family to head for the North Star.

2. CROSSING OVER JORDAN

Among Lewis Hayden's acquaintances in Lexington was a schoolteacher by the name of Delia Webster. A native of Vermont, Webster operated a "female academy," a school for girls. Hayden probably knew her as a regular customer in Brennan's restaurant. In early September 1844, Webster introduced Hayden to her friend, Calvin Fairbank, a minister from Ohio.

Fairbank struck up a conversation with Hayden and said he knew some runaway slaves in Ohio, including one from Lexington. The minister asked Hayden if he would like to be free. When Hayden answered that he would, Fairbank asked a second question.

"But why do you want your freedom, Lewis?"

"Because I'm a man," was the slave's only reply.[1]

In reality, Fairbank was a ministerial student from a college in Ohio. His purpose in Lexington, however, was not innocent. He was there to help slaves escape to freedom.

Fairbank had already helped slaves from Kentucky, Tennessee, and Virginia reach the free states. In his adventures, he had learned that slaves often referred to crossing the Ohio River from

Kentucky to the free state of Ohio as "crossing over Jordan." Just as the tribes of Israel in the Bible crossed over the Jordan River to reach their "Promised Land," many slaves hoped to cross the Ohio River to a "Promised Land" where slavery was forbidden.

Before his trip to Lexington, Fairbank had been a student at Oberlin College in northern Ohio. Just before the start of the fall term in 1844, John Mifflin Brown, an Oberlin student of African descent, asked Fairbank to rescue the wife and children of Gilson Berry, a slave who had recently escaped from Lexington. Fairbank didn't have money for the trip, but Berry claimed he had left money with friends in Lexington that Fairbank could use for his expenses.

Fairbank went to Lexington as requested, but Berry's wife failed to show for a meeting and Berry's friends denied any knowledge of the money. Fairbank was broke and his trip was a failure—until he met Lewis Hayden.

After being introduced by Delia Webster, Hayden and Fairbank held a secret meeting. Fairbank was willing to help Hayden escape, but he explained that he had no money for the expenses. Hayden had money, but insisted he would not head north without his wife and son. Fairbank agreed to work on a plan.

Sizing up his new partner, Fairbank admired Hayden. Here was a slave who had money and who would not leave without his family. "He's worth ten of Berry," thought Fairbank.[2]

Hayden and Fairbank chose Saturday, September 28, for the escape. The date was two days before the expiration of Hayden's contract and, since most slaves were not required to work on Sundays, the Haydens would be safely across the Ohio River before they were missed on Monday morning.

With Hayden's money, Fairbank hired a horse and traveled north, studying the best route for the escape. Sixty-five miles from

Lexington, he reached Maysville, Kentucky, on the south bank of the Ohio River. Fairbank crossed the river on a ferry, then went 8 miles west to Ripley, Ohio, a small town known for its assistance to fugitive slaves. In Ripley, Fairbank recognized a man he had seen crossing the river and learned he was "Pete Driscol, a spy, a patroller, whose business was the detection, and if possible the capture of fugitive slaves." Fairbank asked Driscol about the most likely stops for fugitives. The slave hunter described Ripley as "a black, dirty, abolition hole" where runaways could find assistance at John Rankin's home at the top of the bluff and at Eli Collins's home along the river.

Using this information, Fairbank visited Rankin and Collins, but neighbors had seen him talking to Driscol and had given the warning that Fairbank might be a slave hunter as well. The young minister received a cool welcome at the Rankin home and was almost thrown out of the Collins's house by a son before the elder Collins agreed not to judge his visitor "until the time comes."[3]

Having made his contacts in Ohio, Fairbank returned to Kentucky to finalize the plot. In Lexington, he reserved a carriage and a driver for the last weekend of September, saying he planned to elope to Ohio with Miss Webster.

On September 24, Fairbank wrote a secret report to a friend at Oberlin:

> You may give up the idea of Berry's wife; but I shall bring out three, the father and mother and son, or I am a state prisoner . . . I look on my future prospects and my duty. I look at the worth of my time and my life. I look at its worthlessness if caught; if killed even more so. Friend I shall meet it!! Something will be the result next Sabbath![4]

Rain began on Friday evening, September 27, and continued through Saturday. On Saturday evening, Hayden was probably busy at the Phoenix Hotel, waiting on diners as they celebrated the last day of Lexington's fall race meet. About seven o'clock in the evening, Hayden slipped out of the restaurant and started for the home of Patterson Bain where Harriet and Joseph waited.

Walking through the rain, Hayden crossed a muddy street and approached the Bain house. After assuring himself that no witnesses were in sight, he went to the rear of the house and knocked on a window.

Harriet opened the window and passed seven-year-old Joseph silently into Lewis's arms. Then Lewis helped Harriet climb through the opening. Almost on cue, a carriage drawn by two horses emerged from the dusk and rattled to a halt in front of the Haydens. Calvin Fairbank and Delia Webster were inside. The Haydens climbed in and the driver turned the horses to the north.

In addition to the Haydens, a fourth slave was making the journey. Assigned by his master as driver, Israel cracked his whip and pushed the horses hard, knowing there would be serious consequences for all if they were caught.

Israel guided the carriage along the Maysville Road, the favorite route of Lexingtonians headed north. The first 20 mile section, from Lexington to Paris, Kentucky, was called the "artificial road" as it had been designed by engineers. The artificial road was relatively straight and dry, but the 45 mile stretch from Paris north to the Ohio River followed an old buffalo trail over rugged hilltops and down through muddy creek beds.

Along the road, thirteen tollhouses were spaced at 5-mile intervals. Each tollhouse was a checkpoint where inquisitive toll collectors could peer into carriages to see who was going where. Fairbank suggested that in times of danger Lewis and Harriet could

Calvin Fairbank

Calvin Fairbank first met runaway slaves as a boy, at a religious revival meeting in his home state of New York. His family had traveled to a nearby town for the meeting and was assigned to spend the night in the "good clean home of a pair of escaped slaves." Sitting by the fire in that cabin, young Fairbank heard the former slaves' story of thirty years of abuse. Later that evening the youth pledged to his father, "When I get bigger, they shall not do that."[5]

As Fairbank "got bigger" he reached the conclusion that slavery was a sin and the defeat of slavery became an important part of his personal salvation.

By 1844, when he met Lewis Hayden, Fairbank had helped forty-one slaves escape to the free states north of the Ohio River. In some cases, he merely provided a boat ride across the river. In other cases he was a "Moses," secretly leading families from as far south as Tennessee north to freedom. In one instance, he used money provided by anti-slavery allies to buy a young slave woman at a public auction, in order to prevent her being sold into prostitution.

When Fairbank visited Oberlin College in northern Ohio, the college had a reputation as a radical institution. At a time when few colleges admitted students other than white males, Oberlin admitted men and women, regardless of race. In addition, almost all Oberlin students were abolitionists; that is, they were committed to abolishing slavery immediately. In

By permission of Archive Photos

the summer of 1844, Fairbank enthusiastically enrolled at Oberlin College.

Fairbank was waiting for the fall term to begin, when John Mifflin Brown introduced him to the escaped slave Gilson Berry and asked him to rescue Berry's family. In addition, someone at Oberlin, possibly Brown, gave Fairbank the name of a Lexington schoolteacher who had studied briefly at the college. Her name was Delia Webster.

A Kentucky tollhouse. The Hayden escape party had to pass through thirteen similar gates on their flight from Lexington to Maysville. Courtesy of Archives and Special Collections, University of Kentucky Libraries

be disguised as white travelers by covering their faces with a cloak or a veil or they could pretend to be Delia's servants, while Joseph could hide under the seat.

In the dark carriage the passengers could barely see one another.

"Where are we going?" asked Joseph.

"We're going to freedom," answered his father.

"But where are we going? What town?"

Fairbank replied, "When we get across the river we'll put you on the 'Underground Railroad' bound for Oberlin, Ohio."

"We're going on a train?" Joseph obviously thought a train ride would be a wonderful experience.

"Not a real railroad, a secret railroad," explained Fairbank. "You'll ride in wagons and on horses, but everyone talks as if it were a railroad. The places where you'll hide are called 'stations' and the men and women who run them are 'stationmasters,'"

The minister's voice came out of the dark. "The people who will take you from station to station are called 'conductors,' just like a real railroad. Sometimes they will refer to you, Joseph, as 'a small package' or 'a small box.' Those are code words we use to keep everything a secret."

"But we'll be free once we get across the river, won't we?" asked Harriet.

"No," answered Lewis. "As long as we're in the United States, we won't be truly free."

"Lewis is right," added Fairbank. "Even if you are in a state that forbids slavery, the slavehunters can capture you and return you to Kentucky. You won't be totally free until you reach Canada."

Delia Webster broke in, "When you get to Oberlin, ask for our friend, John Mifflin Brown. You can rest at Oberlin and then Brown will help you get to Canada."

The carriage passed through Paris without incident. Ten miles beyond Paris was Millersburg, the halfway point of the trip. But before the group could reach Millersburg disaster struck. The horses labored to pull the carriage uphill and even in stretches of good road progress was slow.

Fairbank spoke to Israel. They had a serious problem: one of the horses was sick and could not make it to Maysville. A substitute would have to be found at Millersburg. Fairbank and Hayden knew if another horse could not be found, the mission would be doomed.

The fugitives reached Millersburg at midnight. Israel stopped

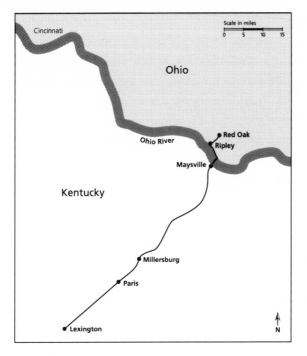

Route of the Hayden family from Lexington to Red Oak, Ohio. Map by Cheryl Conrad

the carriage in front of a darkened hotel. Lewis and Harriet prepared their disguises. Joseph moved to the floor, ready to slip under the seat. Fairbank climbed out of the carriage to find assistance.

The hotel keeper brought out a pitcher of water and examined the horse. Inside the carriage, the passengers passed the time playing a dice game called "Yankee." Since this was a popular game among New England travelers, Delia Webster may have provided the dice and taught the Hayden family the rules.

Finally, after an hour and a half, a new horse was found and hitched to the traces. The carriage started again. The passengers breathed a sigh of relief, but seven tollhouses remained between them and the Ohio River—seven chances for discovery. In addition, the delay meant they would have to cross the Ohio River in daylight, not in the predawn hours as Hayden and Fairbank had planned.

The Haydens and their friends reached the ferry landing at Maysville shortly after dawn Sunday morning. The group was nervous: a passenger and two ferrymen waited on the flatboat. All three were potential witnesses. Would one of them be willing to report the contents of the carriage to a slave hunter for a cash reward?

The fugitives had no choice. The driver guided the horses down the sloped bank and up onto the flatboat. As soon as the boat had left the Kentucky shore, Fairbank emerged from the carriage to pay the ferrymen, probably using Hayden's money. As Fairbank stood on the deck, the ferrymen and the passenger each peered into the carriage through the open door. What did they see? The three witnesses later gave legal affidavits describing Fairbank's group, saying they "saw no persons [in the carriage] but white persons, nor about the carriage but the driver, and he was black."[6]

Did the three men lie in order to cover up the escape? Possibly. But there may be another explanation. Perhaps the three men did not see Joseph, hidden under the seat as Fairbank had recommended. They may have seen only two women. One was Delia Webster, a "white person." The other woman, with her face covered by a veil, they may have assumed was also white. But where was Hayden? Perhaps the hired driver Israel was left hidden on the Kentucky side of the river and consequently the black driver, diligently noted by all three observers, was actually Lewis Hayden.

Once across the river, the group headed west toward Ripley and the home of Eli Collins. Eli's sons must have been stunned to see

Fairbank arrive on Sunday morning with three "packages" ready for delivery to the Underground Railroad.

Webster remained with the Collins family while one of the Collins boys guided Fairbank and the Haydens to a farm at Red Oak, 4 miles north. Here, Calvin Fairbank bade farewell to Lewis, Harriet, and Joseph.

Less than twenty-four hours earlier the Haydens had been slaves in the center of a slave state. Now they were among friends in a free state. They had crossed over Jordan. Although they were still in danger of capture by slave hunters, the most dangerous part of the journey was behind them.

Unfortunately for Israel, Delia Webster, and Calvin Fairbank, the most dangerous part of their journey was still to come with their return to Lexington.

3. HEADED FOR THE NORTH STAR

On Sunday morning, September 29, 1844, Lewis, Harriet, and Joseph Hayden stood in a farmyard in the free state of Ohio, 250 miles south of the Canadian border. As hundreds of fugitives had done before them, and with the help of the stationmasters and the conductors of the Underground Railroad, the Haydens were headed for the North Star that led to Canada and freedom.

Few generalizations can be made about the men and women of the Underground Railroad. Some were black; some were white. Some were farmers; some were town folk. Some were Quakers; others were Methodists or Presbyterians; some followed no formal religion. If the stationmasters and conductors shared one characteristic, it was the courage to ignore the law and defy the slave hunters.

According to federal law, escaped slaves remained the property of their owners, even in a state that did not permit slavery. While the law did not require citizens or local officials to capture fugitives in their area (at least not until 1850) it did allow slaveowners to use force to recover escaped "property" in any state, slave or free.

The greatest danger to escaped slaves and their friends, therefore, was not from local or state officials, but from slave hunters hired by slaveowners. These slave hunters were well armed, rough men interested in capturing escaped slaves to earn cash rewards. They were professionals in their trade, knowing many of the stations along the route north.

The trip from the Ohio River to the shore of Lake Erie must have been a blur to the fugitives who made it. Hiding from the slave hunters, they rested by day and traveled by night, seeing their surroundings only by the light of the moon. They spent each day with a different family and had no map or compass to indicate how far or in what direction they had traveled.

According to Calvin Fairbank, after passing through Ripley, he went "four miles back to Hopkins', where I left the Hayden family."[1] This was the crossroads known as Red Oak, a small community dominated by abolitionists and by the family of Archibald Hopkins. Originally from Virginia, Hopkins had moved his family from Kentucky to Red Oak, Ohio, in 1805. Like almost everyone else in Red Oak, the members of the Hopkins family were eager participants in Underground Railroad activities. In 1844 Archibald was eighty-four years old, so the duty of guiding the Haydens probably fell to one of his eight sons, most likely Gordon, one of the most active of Red Oak's many conductors.

Hopkins followed Fairbank's plan and put the Hayden family on the Underground Railroad bound for Oberlin College, but no record exists of their journey after leaving Red Oak. Lewis Hayden never recorded his family's route and few of the stationmasters and conductors recorded the names of their passengers. We do know, however, the names of many of Ohio's stationmasters and conductors as well as some of the routes and techniques they used.

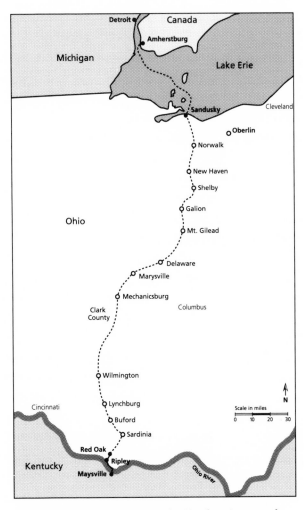

Crossing over the Ohio River, the Haydens journeyed
north to Lake Erie, and then to Amherstburg, Canada.
Depicted is a possible route: all towns along it were
centers of Underground Railroad activity.
Map by Cheryl Conrad

Leaving Red Oak at night, Hopkins probably drove the Haydens to Sardinia, approximately 20 miles north. At Sardinia, local abolitionists paid John W. Hudson, an emancipated slave, to serve as conductor. If the Haydens were entrusted to Hudson, he probably took them along his favorite route, 6 miles northwest to Buford, then a dozen miles north to Lynchburg.

Farther north, the Haydens might have climbed into Jonathan Peirce's false-bottomed wagon. Peirce and his sons picked up fugitives in Wilmington and carried them 18 miles to the Peirce home in Clark County. After the passengers had rested, the Peirce family carried them another 25 miles to Mechanicsburg.

At Mechanicsburg, the Haydens may have hidden in Joseph Ware's intricate cellar called the "Catacombs." Hayden later told friends that his family rode in a wagon, hidden beneath a load of hay, for a portion of their journey. Ware often hid his passengers under a load of hay as he hauled them ten miles to the next station at North Lewisburg.

After three weeks on the trail, the Hayden family eventually reached a Quaker settlement over 200 miles from Red Oak and only a single night's journey from Oberlin College.

In the half light of dawn, the Haydens could see a well tended yard around a modest farmhouse. As Lewis and Harriet walked stiffly from the wagon to the house they could feel the cold air typical of northern Ohio in late October. Lewis carried Joseph, still sleeping. Their guide knocked on the farmhouse door. A woman quickly opened from inside.

"Mr. and Mrs. Hayden, welcome. We have been waiting for thee."

The Haydens could smell breakfast cooking, but their hostess guided them to the parlor.

"Thee has a visitor. He also has been waiting."

Lewis was stunned. Not only did the stationmaster know the Haydens' names, someone was waiting for them.

As the Haydens entered the parlor they saw a young man of African descent seated opposite the window. The mysterious visitor rose to introduce himself and extended his hand.

"Lewis, Harriet, I've come from Oberlin College."

Harriet gasped, then lunged forward to hug him. Lewis, still holding Joseph, extended a firm handshake. *"We have much to thank you for."*

"Your thanks are owed to Calvin Fairbank and Delia Webster, but I'm afraid I bring bad news. Please sit down."

By this time, Joseph was awake. The farm wife led him to breakfast, while the visitor continued.

"When Fairbank and Webster returned to Lexington all was chaos. Every slaveowner in town was sure they had 'stolen' you, as the slaveowners call it. Fairbank and Webster were arrested immediately."

Harriet put her hand to her mouth. Lewis reached for her other hand.

"Are they safe?" asked Lewis.

"There was some talk of lynching, but Delia and Calvin are now in jail waiting for a trial. Calvin was treated roughly, but he's all right. Your driver, Israel, was severely whipped and confessed all. Fortunately for Delia and Calvin, because Israel is a slave his testimony will not be admitted in court."

For the first time, Harriet started to cry. *"Poor Israel, he had nothing to do with this."*

"I'm afraid it gets worse," said the visitor. *"They found a letter in Calvin's pocket addressed to his friends at Oberlin and a letter in Delia's luggage from John Mifflin Brown. Those letters will*

probably prove them guilty. Calvin could go to prison for fifteen years—five years for each slave he helped escape. Delia could go to prison for twenty years—five years for each of you plus five years for Gilson Berry."

Lewis asked, *"How do you know all this?"*

"Harriet, was your master's name Bain?"

Harriet whispered, *"Yes."*

"Bain has hired two slave hunters to capture you and Joseph and bring you back. When they found you had already crossed the river at Maysville, the slave hunters went straight to Oberlin."

The messenger looked directly at Lewis, then at Harriet. *"They're waiting for you at Oberlin. They were looking for Brown as well, but he slipped out of the college."*

Lewis was filled with questions, but he asked only two: *"What can we do to help Delia and Calvin? Where do we go now?"*

"There's nothing we can do to help our friends, except pray. As for the rest of your journey, let's talk about that over breakfast."

Hot coffee and hot biscuits greeted them in the kitchen. Food that had smelled so tantalizing when they first arrived, now held little interest for Lewis and Harriet. Joseph climbed into his mother's lap.

Their hostess set out the route. *"Thee must go to Sandusky, twenty miles north of here. From there, thee can catch a steamer across Lake Erie to Canada."*

"What about Brown? Will he be captured?" asked Lewis.

"I don't believe so. He never was a slave. He was born free. Even if the slave hunters find him, they have no legal rights over him."

"Brown's going to be acting pastor of a church in Detroit. He has friends there. You had better stay in Canada for a while," cautioned the messenger. *"But when it's safe, I am sure he would be*

pleased to have you join him."

"When do we leave?" asked Lewis.

"As soon as thee has finished thy breakfast," answered their hostess from across the room. "There is no use waiting for the slave hunters to come looking for thee. My husband and son are hitching the team now."

Warned not to continue their journey to Oberlin, the Haydens turned north toward Sandusky. There they could have hidden in the homes of a dozen stationmasters, many of them black. One of the busiest stations was the home of Thomas Holland Boston, a black Methodist preacher, who moved into Sandusky only a year before the Haydens' escape. When his home was filled to capacity, Boston convinced his neighbors to accept fugitives. Just down the street from Reverend Boston, escapees waiting for a sympathetic steamboat captain often hid in a barn owned by Dr. Tilden.

According to their plan, the Haydens boarded a steamboat for the trip across Lake Erie to Canada, a land where slavery was forbidden and American fugitives were protected under the flag of the British Empire. The Haydens disembarked in Canada at the town of Amherstburg, a popular destination for escaped slaves. Amherstburg was separated from the state of Michigan by only the width of the Detroit River.

Despite its proximity to the United States, Amherstburg offered valuable resources for the fugitives. The most visible resources, ones that must have been immensely reassuring to the illegal emigrants, were the cannons of nearby Fort Malden, pointed directly at the American shore.

A few years before Hayden's arrival, British officials had revitalized Fort Malden in order to respond to a rebellion in that part of Canada. Touring the fortress in October 1844, Lewis Hayden saw it at the peak of its strength. As he walked along the earth-works that formed the walls of the garrison, Hayden admired the "solid regular-angle piles of cannon balls" and mused that "Old John Bull's blue pills," the British cannonballs, might be the final cure for the illness of American slavery.[2]

Yet Amherstburg had resources for the fugitives far more valuable than cannonballs. One of the first persons the Haydens met as they stepped off the boat was a thin man with rotten teeth and tattered clothes named Isaac Rice. Formerly a Presbyterian minister in Ohio, Rice was a dedicated worker in the anti-slavery cause. Through his Union Border Mission, Rice was a self-appointed supply master to the fugitives, offering food, clothing, and even schooling.

Rice believed blacks and whites should live together—not always a popular stance even with those opposed to slavery. As evidence of his belief, Rice lived in a shack among Amherstburg's black population and he maintained a sick room in his home for those needing care.

As talented as he was in assisting fugitives, Rice also had a talent for making enemies. He had no patience with the anti-slavery societies that supported him, and he often refused to submit the reports they required. He was also woefully inadequate as a financial manager and his constant begging for the "poor degenerate fugitives" earned his mission the title of "the Begging Society," embarrassing the families it assisted.[3]

Despite his shortcomings, Rice impressed Hayden as one of the martyrs of the cause. Hayden would eventually collect money on the missionary's behalf and would write friends:

> [Rice] is struggling untiringly, unyieldingly. I hope he
> may not lack as formerly for means to carry on effective

war against all oppression. He has stood 7 years alone, and often faint for food. If he refuses to quit the field, as he never would, may the love of his friends stand by. I am willing to say he is near to my heart.[4]

Before leaving Amherstburg, Hayden had one task he wished to accomplish. He wanted to write a letter to Lewis Baxter, one of his former owners. Although able to read some, Hayden was unable to write effectively and hired an amanuensis (a professional secretary) to record his dictation. The letter was written exactly four weeks after the Haydens crossed the Ohio River and indicates the family had been in Amherstburg at least a few days, since Lewis and Joseph were already attending school. The letter contains irony, sarcasm, a reference to the seventeenth century philosopher, John Locke, and a strong vocabulary—a remarkable letter from an unschooled fugitive slave.

Finally, Hayden sarcastically signed the letter, "your affectionate friend, Lewis Hayden." Realizing that his former master might not recognize him by his family name, he crossed out "Hayden" and wrote "Grant," the name his co-owners, Baxter and Grant, had given him. In this letter, Lewis Hayden used his slave name for the last time.[5]

Amherstburg October 27, 1844

Mr. Baxter,

Sir you have already discovered me absent. This will give you notice where and why—I never was a great friend to the institution of robbing and crushing slavery and have finally become sick of the whole concern and have concluded for the present to try my freedom and how it will seam [sic] to be my own master and manage my own matters and crack my own whip.

. . . I also at length concluded to try how it will seem to walk about like a gentleman, my share of the time I am willing to labor but am also desirous to act the gentleman with all the important mien that attaches to a man who is indeed a truth, himself, the self, identical to the very living Being of whom Locke wrote in his essays.

I may not, even though a Freeman, expect at this late date to become familiar with the Arts and Sciences as if I had never been robbed and even now I have to get an amanuensis to pen down my broken, irregular and incoherent thoughts but I am now sitting with writing implements in my hand and have been already at school and mean to go more and my little son is going to school and I intend shall be able to write his own pen at the instance and impulse of his swelling soul. . . .

So farewell—Any communication after this had best be sent to the British North American Institute on River Sydenham, the Colored People's College.

. . . your affectionate friend,

Lewis ~~Hayden~~ Grant

4. HIS OWN MASTER

In his letter to his former master, Lewis Hayden wrote that he could be contacted at the "British North American Institute on River Sydenham, the Colored People's College." This institute, sometimes called the "Dawn Settlement," was located near Dresden, Ontario, about 75 miles northeast of Amherstburg.

Josiah Henson and Hiram Wilson established the Dawn Settlement in 1842, just two years before the arrival of the Hayden family. Henson, a former slave in Maryland and Kentucky, had been in Canada since escaping with his family in 1830. Wilson, a former ministerial student at Oberlin College, arrived in Canada in 1836, intending to work as a missionary among the fugitives. Henson and Wilson operated their institute as a manual training school, as an adult education center, and as a communal settlement where former slaves could adjust to the requirements of a free life.

Unfortunately, there is no record that the Haydens ever participated in the activities at Dawn. Apparently, the isolation of a farm community in the Canadian wilderness held little appeal for Hayden. In addition, even though he had obtained freedom for himself and his family, Hayden heard an appeal from within to return to the United States and take an active role in the struggle to end slavery. After only a few months in Canada, the Haydens crossed the Detroit River and returned to the United States via the city of Detroit.

Despite their status as fugitive slaves, Lewis and Harriet may have felt they could safely move to Detroit in the spring of 1845 because events in Lexington had brought some resolution to their escape. These events, however, were as unfortunate for Delia Webster and Calvin Fairbank as they were helpful for the Haydens.

The Haydens' escape had created a sensation. Most slaves who were able to escape did so on the basis of their own wits and their own courage. Assistance from non-slaves, white or black, was usually not available until the escapees had reached a free state. In the Hayden case a white man and a white woman had escorted an entire slave family 65 miles in a rented carriage with a hired driver. Slaveowners realized Fairbank and Webster had created a dangerous precedent: their crimes were serious.

Webster was jailed in Lexington from her capture on September 30, 1844 until her trial in late December. Represented by three of Lexington's best-known attorneys, she was found guilty of conspiring with Fairbank. The charges of assisting Lewis, Harriet, and Joseph in their escape were set aside and were not decided. She was sentenced to two years in prison and began serving her sentence at the Kentucky Penitentiary in Frankfort on January 10, 1845.

Fairbank's trial was held in February. On the first day of the trial, the young minister pleaded guilty to the "abduction" of Joseph, Harriet, and Lewis Hayden, and was sentenced to fifteen years in prison. Fairbank did not obtain a reduced sentence by admitting his guilt, but apparently he did gain leniency for Webster. On February

24, less than two weeks after Fairbank's sentencing, the governor of Kentucky pardoned Webster. The schoolteacher promptly returned to her home in Vermont.

Even in Canada, Lewis and Harriet could follow the trials of Webster and Fairbank from reports in the newspapers and in anti-slavery publications. With Fairbank in prison, Webster safely in Vermont, and the slave hunters back in Kentucky, the Haydens felt sufficiently safe to return to the United States—as long as they stayed away from the Kentucky-Ohio border.

When Hayden reached Detroit in the spring of 1845, he joined forces with John Mifflin Brown, the black ministerial student who had sent Fairbank on his fateful trip to Lexington. As acting pastor, Brown was trying to build a congregation of the African Methodist Episcopal Church. His first goal was to replace the congregation's temporary wooden building with a permanent brick structure.

Hayden helped Brown raise money for the new church. Through their efforts, on June 5, 1845, a site was purchased for $300 for the first permanent home of Detroit's Bethel African Methodist Episcopal Church. Seven hundred dollars were still needed to construct the building, so in the fall Brown and Hayden traveled east to raise money from supporters of the anti-slavery movement in Boston, Massachusetts.

Boston was the center of American anti-slavery activity. In Boston, the Reverend Theodore Parker, grandson of a hero of the American Revolution, preached against the sin of slavery. Wendell Phillips, one of America's greatest orators and the son of a Boston mayor, railed against slavery as corrupting "the very air we breathe."[1] Maria Weston Chapman, a descendant of Pilgrims and secretary of the American Anti-Slavery Society, sent out "agents" from Boston to deliver the anti-slavery message to every town in New York and New England.

These radicals were not just opposed to slavery. They opposed colonization (favored by Henry Clay) and they opposed the gradual emancipation of the slaves. Like the students and faculty at Oberlin College, they would only be satisfied with the immediate abolition of slavery. Consequently, they were called "abolitionists."

The leader of the abolitionists in New England, many of them wealthy blue bloods, was a newspaper editor of modest means who had been raised in a poor family. William Lloyd Garrison published the *Liberator* each week in Boston and his name and the name of his newspaper were synonymous with the abolition movement.

When Brown and Hayden arrived in Boston in 1845, Garrison was not only the publisher of the *Liberator*, but he was also the president and guiding force of the American Anti-Slavery Society. The Society's office on Cornhill Street was one of the first stops in Boston for Brown and Hayden. Society members gave the visitors a warm welcome and gathered around to hear the reports on the conditions of fugitive slaves in Detroit and across the river in Canada. Hayden also related stories of his life as a slave and of his dramatic escape from Kentucky.

Among the listeners was John A. Andrew, a young lawyer. Hayden and Andrew quickly became friends and would remain friends for the rest of their lives. Andrew would eventually become involved in politics and be elected governor of Massachusetts. As his political success grew, Hayden became one of his closest allies.

While in Massachusetts, Hayden attended his first anti-slavery conventions. These mass meetings were an important part of the work of the American Anti-Slavery Society. Without the benefit of telephone, radio, or television the Society relied on these meetings to inform and energize its members. At the meetings speakers would inflame the audience by talking about the brutality of slavery. Other speakers would call for passage of resolutions against slavery or against a host of slavery-related issues, such as ministers who owned slaves or ministers who refused to label slavery as a sin. While the passage of the resolutions was usually a foregone conclusion, the act of voting for them was one more step in getting total commitment from the Society's followers.

On the first day of October 1845, just one year after his escape, Hayden attended an anti-slavery convention in Boston. When it was rumored that Hayden's former owner might be at the convention trying to recapture his escaped slave, a speaker rose from the audience and suggested any slave hunter with "design of interfering with the personal liberty of Mr. Hayden" should immediately obtain a life insurance policy. Hayden appeared briefly before the convention and was not molested.[2]

By November, Hayden and Brown had gathered $163 to send back to Detroit. They sent another $150 at the end of December and $100 in January 1846. (These amounts may seem small, but at that time a skilled laborer was grateful to earn $50 a month.) On March 6, 1846, the *Liberator* published a letter from Ross Wilkins, the United States district judge for the District of Michigan, acknowledging the contributions. Wilkins, described by the *Liberator* as "a warm friend of the colored people," reported the church building was sufficiently complete for Sunday school classes to meet in the basement while work continued on the upper story. With less than $300 to go to their goal, Hayden and Brown made plans to return to Detroit.

Some of Hayden's new friends, however, recommended he become a speaker for the American Anti-Slavery Society as the former slave Frederick Douglass had done. At the suggestion of his

William Lloyd Garrison

William Lloyd Garrison had a background that was in some respects closer to the lives of the slaves he was trying to rescue than the privileged lives of the reformers who followed him. His father ran off before Lloyd was three years old and Garrison began life in a family so poor he sometimes had to take an empty pail to a nearby mansion to beg for scraps of food. (Slaves were well aware of such leftovers. "Pot-lickings" were considered a benefit of being a house slave rather than a field hand.)

At age thirteen, Garrison was apprenticed to a newspaper editor. During the seven years of his apprenticeship, he developed a firm command of language in addition to skill in typesetting. The young printer also developed a hatred of slavery. When he launched his own weekly newspaper, in 1831, he called it the *Liberator* and dedicated it to the defeat of slavery.

In the first issue of the *Liberator*, Garrison rejected the gradual emancipation of slaves, as supported by many reformers, and called for the immediate abolition of slavery in the United States. Without regard for public opinion, he vowed, "I will be as harsh as truth, and as uncompromising as justice . . . I will not excuse—I will not retreat a single inch—AND I WILL BE HEARD."

As determined as he was to defeat slavery, Garrison was equally determined that the victory would not be a bloody one. He believed slavery was a sin, but he also believed vio-

By permission of the American Antiquarian Society

lence was a sin. Garrison was not a coward. He often spoke before hostile audiences. But he was as anti-violence as he was anti-slavery. He believed the sin of slavery could only be defeated by "moral suasion," that is, by a moral conversion of the nation.

In the most extreme version of his doctrine, Garrison was opposed to any form of participation in a government that permitted slavery. This philosophy included a ban on voting in public elections, even if the vote was in favor of an anti-slavery candidate. Garrison reasoned that since the Constitution and the government of the United States permitted slavery, the Constitution and the government were evil. According to Garrison and his loyal followers, participation within a system that condoned slavery was participation in slavery itself.

Garrison published the *Liberator* from January 1831 to December 1865. The single sheet, four-page weekly newspaper never had more than two to three thousand subscribers. But for thirty-five years it was the bible of the abolition movement in the United States, and William Lloyd Garrison was its prophet.

friends, Hayden attended an anti-slavery convention in Watertown, Massachusetts, on March 19, 1846, and opened that meeting by giving an "account of his escape from bondage."[3]

The next day, Hayden attended an anti-slavery convention in New Bedford, Massachusetts. One of the first resolutions before the convention included language that "So long as the people of the North give places of honor and emolument [advantage] to slaveholders . . . [the Northerners] are equally with the South involved in the guilt of slavery, and are in fact slaveholders." According to the *Liberator*, Hayden made some remarks concerning the resolutions. Although the subject of his remarks was not recorded, the former slave was in good company. Other speakers at the convention were Garrison and a wealthy black with a long record of anti-slavery speaking, Charles Lenox Remond.[4]

Hayden was so moved by the anti-slavery conventions he wrote to a friend, "On looking over the vast assembly, and hearing the expressions of sympathy and encouragement from the speakers, I forgot myself, and felt for a time that I was in Paradise. But on hearing the wrongs of slavery portrayed my joy was turned into sorrow."[5]

On March 31, Hayden left for Detroit by way of New York City. At Garrison's request, he carried a letter from Garrison to Sydney Howard Gay, editor of the *National Anti-Slavery Standard*, the official publication of the American Anti-Slavery Society. In the letter, Garrison gave his appraisal of Lewis Hayden:

> Lewis has won the esteem and friendship of all with whom he has become acquainted, and is a rare young man. Should he conclude to return, and take up his abide [*sic*] in New Bedford, I think he can be made very serviceable to our cause. He needs to be more with us,

fully to understand the position that we occupy, in regard to Church and State; but he is an apt scholar; and
has made very good progress in a very short time. I have
not had a good opportunity to hear him speak in public;
but I believe he has generally acquitted himself to good
acceptance. His chief embarrassment seems to be, to
find language to express the facts of his history, and the
thoughts and emotions of his mind.[6]

After returning to Detroit, Hayden was restless. He had seen the
important work done by the American Anti-Slavery Society and he
wanted to be a part of it. Frederick Douglass had been "on the
platform," speaking to anti-slavery audiences, for almost five
years. William Wells Brown, like Hayden an escaped slave from
Kentucky, was also speaking about his experiences and against
slavery. Why couldn't Hayden join this group?

Maria Weston Chapman had an important role in choosing the
agents who would speak on behalf of the Society. She was also
their field supervisor. She handed out their allowances of seven or
eight dollars a week. She reproached them when they failed to
properly represent the Society. She was the person Hayden had to
impress.

Hayden wrote a long letter to Chapman in May 1846.
Addressing her as "Dear Sister," he gave a moving report on the results of his efforts in Detroit. "All classes, rich, poor, all colors as-
semble in our unfinished church. Prejudice vanishes, the gospell
[sic] gains ground. Light is breaking in on us." The letter included
a long and impassioned plea for the efforts of Isaac Rice in Canada,
and requested that Chapman show the letter to "Friend Garrison."

As for as his own activities, Hayden reported, or perhaps

boasted, "I should have been East now but for an invitation to visit and take up collections in some of the popular churches of this city." He concluded with an apology for being unable to attend the annual May meeting of the American Anti-Slavery Society that year, but still promoting himself as an effective speaker declared that, "the invitations of this city forbid."[7]

Hayden returned to Boston and throughout the summer of 1846 continued his campaign to be named an anti-slavery agent. In July, Edmund Quincy (another Boston blue blood opposed to slavery) wrote Chapman on Hayden's behalf: "Has anything been done about Lewis Hayden's credentials as Agent? I told him it should be done."[8]

On the first of August, Hayden attended a "meeting in a fine grove" just outside Concord, Massachusetts. The purpose of the meeting was to celebrate the anniversary of the end of slavery in the British West Indies. The crowd was small, but the weather was pleasant and the speakers were noteworthy. According to a report in the *Liberator* on August 7, Channing (probably Ellery, nephew and namesake of the famous clergyman, William Ellery Channing) reviewed the progress of the anti-slavery campaign over the past year. Ralph Waldo Emerson followed and was "calm" and "philosophical" telling "the need be of all things." Hayden followed Emerson, but made a strong impression, "stammering out touchingly, that which none has power fully to utter, what a glorious thing liberty is."

Hayden probably met at least one other notable resident of Concord that day. The "fine grove" was located near Walden Pond, and the speakers at the meeting stood on the step of Henry David Thoreau's now-famous cabin. In addition to hosting the event, Thoreau may have been the author of the unsigned summary of the meeting that appeared in the *Liberator*.

By the spring of 1847, Harriet had joined Lewis in Massachusetts and the couple moved to New Bedford, 50 miles south of Boston, as Garrison had recommended. In the 1840s, New Bedford was the one of the wealthiest cities in America, the center of a thriving whaling industry. The town offered plenty of jobs and had a sizable community of blacks. Nine years before the Haydens reached New Bedford, it had been the first home of Frederick Douglass and his wife after their escape from slavery. In New Bedford, Douglass was able to find his first paying jobs as a free man—cutting wood, shoveling coal, and loading and unloading vessels for a dollar a day.

The abolitionists may have recommended New Bedford for a reason that might be called racist 150 years later. In New Bedford, one resident in fifteen was black; in Boston only one person in sixty. The white abolitionists may have felt the Haydens would be happier among "their own kind" in New Bedford.

For the rest of the spring Hayden shuttled back and forth between New Bedford and Boston, keeping up with friends in Detroit and the Dawn Settlement in Canada by letter. Still not accepted by the American Anti-Slavery Society as an authorized representative, Hayden carried on a personal crusade of writing and speaking. On May 8, in a letter to Sydney Gay of the *National Anti-Slavery Standard*, he apologized for missing another annual convention due to a speaking engagement in South Woburn, Massachusetts.

Gay not only published Hayden's letter in the *Standard* on May 20, but had it read to the delegates at the meeting in New York City. Perhaps this letter more than any other describes the motivation that moved Hayden forward, not just toward a new life as a free man, but on a quest to defeat the forces of slavery throughout the nation. In his letter, Hayden recalled his brothers and sisters in slavery and especially his first wife and his son, sold to the slave traders by Henry Clay:

> Sir, while sitting alone in my room, thinking of your meeting, my mind has been led to the South, there gathering together my scattered and chattelized relations, but I cannot find them. O, when shall slavery cease? God speed the day I pray, and when I dare to think or bring to mind one dreadful and terrifying fact, that the wife of my youth, and my first born child, is dragging out a life on some tyrant's plantation. I pray you just look at the condition of my wife, driven all day, under the lash, and then at night to be at the will of any demon or deacon that has a white face. How long shall these things be?

5. On the Road for Freedom

Lewis and Harriet Hayden began the summer of 1847 with a trip to Vermont to visit Delia Webster, their friend from Lexington, at her family's home near Vergennes. The journey from Boston to Vermont was not a pleasant one, however, since the Haydens repeatedly encountered discrimination along the way. On one train the conductor ordered an additional first class car rather than allow the former slaves to sit with other first class passengers. When Lewis and Harriet tried to board a steamboat, the clerk denied them passage until he was reversed by the boat captain. On another steamboat, they were not allowed to eat breakfast with the white passengers. Despite the trouble, the Haydens were warmly welcomed by Delia and her friends and, according to Lewis, "in Vermont, we are received not only with *hospitality*, but with *kindness* and *cordiality*."[1]

In addition to the trip to Vermont, the summer of 1847 was important to Lewis Hayden for another reason: in June the Executive Committee of the American Anti-Slavery Society approved him as an "agent," one of its traveling speakers. Effective August 1, Hayden was to begin touring New York State, preaching the anti-slavery gospel.

Hayden was assigned to travel with Dr. Erasmus Darwin ("E. D.") Hudson. Born in Torrington, Massachusetts in 1806, Hudson received his medical degree in 1827 and established his practice in Connecticut. Hudson was a religious man and ardently opposed the use of alcoholic beverages. At the request of local leaders of the temperance movement, Hudson began lecturing against the consumption of alcohol.

At that time, the anti-alcohol and anti-slavery movements were often related as part of more general efforts for moral and social reform, and Hudson soon added anti-slavery topics to his lectures. In 1838 he set aside his medical practice and devoted his full efforts to the lecture circuit.

Hudson, who was white, was an early friend and companion of Frederick Douglass. The men met in August 1842, a year after Douglass's debut as an anti-slavery speaker. By the end of that year Hudson and Douglass were touring western New York together, speaking against slavery.

Douglass was a remarkable speaker. He began each meeting with tales of his experiences as a slave and his escape by railroad using the false documents of a seaman. He enthralled audiences with dramatic gestures and entertained them with his contemptuous impression of a Southern preacher, calling on slaves to follow St. Paul's command, "Servants, be obedient unto your masters." [2]

Hudson and Douglass traveled through snowstorms and across flooded creeks, but the lectures could be as dangerous as the travel. Not all listeners came with an open mind. Some came to heckle the speakers. Others came prepared to use physical force. During a meeting in Indiana in 1843, a mob attacked Douglass and his fellow speakers. (Hudson was not present.) In the ensuing melee, the ruffians broke Douglass's hand and knocked out the teeth of a white supporter.

Dr. Erasmus Darwin Hudson had traveled with both Frederick Douglass and William Wells Brown for the American Anti-Slavery Society. Hayden paired up with him in 1847. From *History of Torrington, Connecticut* by Samuel Orcutt, 1878. Courtesy of the University of Massachusetts, Amherst

Douglass and Hudson lectured together, on and off, from 1842 until Douglass left for Europe in the summer of 1845. (He would not return until early in 1847.) Hudson resumed his anti-slavery tours in 1846 and continued into 1847 with William Wells Brown. Like Douglass, Brown was a former slave and a talented speaker and writer.

In June 1847, Joseph C. Hathaway, General Agent of the American Anti-Slavery Society for New York, wrote Hudson that "Lewis Hayden (the Fugitive slave) has been engaged & will commence on the first of August & it is proposed to put him with thee if agreeable to thyself."[3]

Hudson was to receive $12 per week plus expenses, provided he would furnish a horse and buggy and take in Hayden or some other traveling companion. Hudson's fee was higher than the seven to eight dollars per week normally paid anti-slavery agents. The increased fee probably was reasonable, however, considering

Hudson's experience and the transportation he supplied.

The American Anti-Slavery Society allowed Hudson to choose the towns he would visit. Once he had selected his itinerary, Hudson was to send the list to the *National Anti-Slavery Standard* so the meetings could be promoted in the paper. On July 29, 1847, the *Standard* announced that "Lewis Hayden, the fugitive slave from Kentucky, and E. D. Hudson, from Massachusetts, Agents of the American Anti-Slavery Society, will hold Anti-Slavery meetings at the following towns. . . ."

The schedule was ambitious. Hudson and Hayden were to make their first appearance on August 2 at Hillsdale, New York, just beyond the Massachusetts-New York state line. On August 3 and 4, they were to be 17 miles farther west, in Hudson. After Hudson, they were to cross the Hudson River and travel another nine miles to Cairo for appearances August 5 and 6.

According to the announcement, Hudson and Hayden would appear in nineteen towns during the month of August. Meetings were scheduled for every evening and most afternoons but there was no public relations specialist to make the arrangements. If local subscribers had not arranged for a hall, Hudson would visit ministers asking for use of a meeting place. If the ministers refused (and they often did, fearing controversy) Hudson would go out in the street seeking a room for the lecture.

In the small towns visited by the anti-slavery agents, traveling speakers were a form of entertainment and the speakers' topic, slavery, was a remote idea. In addition, prior to a visit from Hayden or Douglass many of the rural residents had never seen a person with dark skin. Audiences attended because of curiosity as well as conviction, and the anti-slavery agents were not necessarily disappointed that a significant portion of their listeners were present only for lack of something better to do.

ANTI-SLAVERY MEETINGS IN NEW YORK

Lewis Hayden, the fugitive slave from Kentucky, and E. D. Hudson, from Massachusetts, Agents of the American Anti-Slavery Society, will hold Anti-Slavery meetings at the following towns and villages:

OTSEGO COUNTY

Maple Grove, (Butternuts) Thurs. & Fri. Sept. 9 & 10.

Oneants, Saturday and Sunday, 11 and 12.

Laurensville, (Laurens) Monday and Tuesday, 13 & 14.

Noblesville, Wednesday, 15.

South Edmonton, Thursday, 16.

Burlington Flats, Friday and Saturday, 17 and 18.

MADISON COUNTY

Leonardsville, Sunday, September 19.

North Brookfield, Monday and Tuesday, 20 and 21.

ONEIDA COUNTY

Bridgewater, Wednesday, September 22.

HERKIMER COUNTY

Litchfield, Thursday and Friday, September 23 and 24.

Winfield, Saturday, 25

The meetings will commence at one and seven o'clock, P.M.

Will the friends of the slave make all necessary arrangements in their respective and neighboring towns to have the meetings well notified and attendance enjoined, and confer a favour on the cause of bleeding and imploring humanity.

JOSEPH C. HATHAWAY,
General Agent of American Society for New York

Typical notice for the speaking tour of Lewis Hayden and E. D. Hudson through New York State as announced in the National Anti-Slavery Standard.

In the meetings, Hayden took the role that had belonged to Douglass. He told of the cruelties he had suffered as a slave, and he recounted his dramatic escape with his family. Like Douglass and Brown, Hayden not only educated the audience but gave them a rare glimpse of a former slave. His composed presence helped the audience realize that slaves were not the totally dependent sub-humans often portrayed by pro-slavery forces.

After Hayden finished his personal tale, it would have been Hudson's role to deliver Garrison's doctrine as endorsed by the American Anti-Slavery Society, that slavery was a sin and that since the Constitution of the United States permitted slavery, the Constitution and the government were evil. The Society would also have expected the speakers to endorse Garrison's doctrine of nonviolence (which he called nonresistance) and moral suasion as the methods to free the oppressed.

The agents also performed financial duties. They sold subscriptions for the *National Anti-Slavery Standard* and for the *Liberator* and took up collections to cover their expenses.

Hudson's and Hayden's lectures continued through the fall. At the end of September, they appeared in West Winfield and Little Falls, New York, with Frederick Douglass and William Lloyd Garrison. In October and November they traveled along the southern boundary of the Adirondack Mountains. In early November, Hudson's son was injured in an accident, apparently breaking a leg, and Hayden's mentor rushed home as father and as physician.

Hudson's departure left Hayden to stand alone in Trenton (now Barneveld) for two days of appearances. A minister in the audience later wrote to the *Standard* that Hayden "appeared, chiefly, to tell his own story, and to exhibit the miseries of the system of slavery, as illustrated in his own personal experience." According to the report, Hayden passed over Hudson's role of attacking the Constitution and the government for being pro-slavery, feeling unable to present remarks that would be "satisfactory to himself."

Despite Hayden's limited performance, the minister was astonished that, "with so little early mental cultivation, he should have been able to be so accurate an observer of men and manners." The writer concluded, "The Society which has sent him forth, need not doubt that he will do great good."[4]

When Hudson returned to the tour the pair continued their journey. Fourteen towns were scheduled for December, and by Christmas they had reached Oswego, on the shore of Lake Ontario. Eight more towns were announced for January plus an Anti-Slavery Fair, January 26–27, at West Winfield.

On December 28, Hathaway sent Hudson a letter indicating he was pleased "the [Executive] Committee have decided to retain thee and Lewis in their service." In his letter, Hathaway made suggestions for possible visits in the spring, pointing out that five counties alone could keep Hayden and Hudson busy until May. Showing his affection for Hayden, Hathaway closed the letter with "Make my love to Lewis and believe me."[5]

The trip across New York in December and January must have been as uncomfortable as it was dangerous. Modern winter travel can be treacherous, even with heated automobiles and national weather forecasts. Imagine the challenge for two men traveling 10 to 20 miles a day through a New York winter, in an open carriage, behind a single horse.

Despite the hardships, Hayden continued to get good reviews for his efforts. In January, a correspondent wrote to the *Standard* from Hastings, New York, that, "Lewis Hayden's honesty, simplicity, and position commend him to every heart; while his pathetic appeals for his brethren in bonds, seem sufficient to move a world to the rescue." The former slave did not limit his performances to speeches. At a "Female Anti-Slavery Meeting," Hayden provided "singing and prayer."[6]

But all was not well. In mid-February, Hudson received a letter from Wendell Phillips, who had replaced Maria Weston Chapman as secretary of the American Anti-Slavery Society, terminating Lewis Hayden as an agent. The exact reasons for the termination are unclear. Presumably Hayden was dismissed with Hudson's consent; possibly even on his recommendation. The stated reason for the termination was Hayden's failure as a speaker, but Hayden had been speaking before anti-slavery groups for a year and a half. He had been with Hudson for six months and the Executive Committee had renewed his appointment in December. Certainly it did not take almost 100 public appearances to determine whether the escaped slave was an acceptable public speaker. The reason was probably more complex.

While Hayden succeeded in telling his personal tale, the uneducated former slave might have found it difficult to explain, or even agree with, Garrison's complicated view of the Constitution as a pro-slavery document. The leaders of the Society may have mistakenly attributed Hayden's inability to explain their views on the Constitution to a lack of ability in Hayden, rather than to a flaw in a doctrine Frederick Douglass would publicly reject in 1851.

Hayden might also have publicly disagreed with the American Anti-Slavery Society's philosophy of nonresistance and moral suasion. The patient attitude of Garrison and his disciples (many of them wealthy, most of them white) might have rung hollow for a man who had suffered under slavery and had family members still suffering. Hayden had labored long and hard to become an agent of the American Anti-Slavery Society. His termination as a public speaker may have been the beginning of Hayden's realization that it would take more than speeches and moral suasion to save his "scattered and chattelized relations."

Phillips's letter terminating Hayden does not survive. All that survives is a pitiful letter from Hayden to Phillips, dated February 21, 1848, begging for enough money to return to Detroit. (Apparently Harriet had moved back to Detroit while Lewis was on the road.) Hayden also apologized for his performance as a speaker, pointing out that he was "jest three years from slavery." Writing to the anti-slavery movement's finest orator, Hayden admitted he was not "a second yourself" but promised that "if I am not Wendell Phillips now; it dought not appear what I shall be for I shall not leve one stone unturned to obtain light."[7]

On February 17, the *National Anti-Slavery Standard* published Hudson's schedule for the second half of February. In the announcement, the paper carefully deleted reference to Lewis Hayden and reported only "E. D. Hudson's appointments in company with an American slave in Herkimer, Ostego, and St. Lawrence counties."

6. A New Mission

When Lewis Hayden returned to Detroit in February 1848, he was broke and he was discouraged. As an agent of the American Anti-Slavery Society, he had failed. As a speaker, he was not a Wendell Phillips. Nor was he a Frederick Douglass. But he was determined to find his role in the anti-slavery fight, and in order to find that role he would not "leve one stone unturned."

In order to continue his fight against slavery, Hayden abandoned his efforts in Detroit and moved his family to Boston. A great battle was coming, and Lewis Hayden was determined to be at its center. If he was not to be a speaker on behalf of the anti-slavery movement, he would quickly find a new mission.

In the summer of 1849, Hayden opened a store on Cambridge Street in Boston with, according to his advertisement in the *Liberator*, a "good assortment of Men's and Boy's Clothing."[1] In addition, Lewis and Harriet operated a boardinghouse in their home on Southac Street. These legitimate businesses, however, had a secret purpose.

Through the boardinghouse and the clothing store, Lewis and Harriet provided food, shelter, and clothing for fugitive slaves

The Liberator *announced Hayden's new clothing store in Boston. Like the boardinghouse operated by Lewis and Harriet, this was to become a familiar part of the underground Railroad.* Courtesy of the Trustees of the Boston Public Library traveling north. In their new home, the Haydens had found a new mission as stationmasters on the Boston link of the Underground Railroad. Secondhand clothing from Lewis's store was especially needed since many of the slaves had escaped from southern states with only the clothes they were wearing and were unprepared for New England winters.

The Haydens also had a debt to repay. Early in 1849, Lewis learned that in exchange for $650, his former owners would join in a petition to the governor of Kentucky for the release of Calvin Fairbank. Five years after the Haydens' escape, Fairbank remained in a Kentucky prison for assisting them.

Hayden raised the $650 from 160 donors in less than sixty days and deposited the money with Francis Jackson, treasurer of the *National Anti-Slavery Standard*. Jackson held the money until Fairbank's release on August 24, 1849, then paid the "ransom" to Lewis's former owners.[2]

While Lewis Hayden had a new role in the fight against slavery, events outside Boston were about to turn the fight into a war.

In 1850, a constitutional battle was taking place in the United States Congress in Washington, D.C. The sounds of the battle could be heard throughout the nation. Southern states were threatening to leave the Union unless slavery was protected in the South and allowed to expand into the western territories. Anti-slavery representatives from the North opposed the expansion of slavery and wanted to ban it in the District of Columbia.

Two senators, Henry Clay of Kentucky and Daniel Webster of Massachusetts, promoted a compromise to save the Union. With their support, and leadership from Stephen Douglas of Illinois, Congress passed a series of related laws, known as the Compromise of 1850, that made concessions to both sides:

California was admitted as a free state; slavery was permitted in the new territories of Utah and New Mexico; slave trading was prohibited in the District of Columbia, although owning slaves was still permitted; and a severe fugitive slave law was enacted.

This last measure, the Fugitive Slave Law of 1850, directly affected the Haydens and their friends. Its purpose was to help slaveowners recapture runaway slaves in the free states. The law not only provided a $1,000 fine or six months in prison for anyone assisting a fugitive slave, it required private citizens to assist in the capture of anyone accused of being an escaped slave. According to the law, a person captured and accused of being a fugitive slave would be brought before a federal commissioner. The accused had no right to speak or to present a defense. Upon testimony of the owner, or the owner's representative, the defendant could promptly be returned to slavery.

The anti-slavery forces were especially offended by the plan for compensating commissioners. Under the law, a commissioner would receive $10 if he ruled the defendant was a slave and returned him or her to an owner. If the commissioner found the defendant was not a slave, the fee was only $5. The extra fee for returning the accused to slavery was rationalized as compensation for extra paperwork.

President Millard Fillmore signed the Fugitive Slave Law on September 18, 1850. Within two weeks, an escaped slave was arrested in New York and returned to his owner under the guard of United States marshals. The Compromise of 1850 had turned federal marshals into slave hunters.

Lewis Hayden had paid for his freedom with the $650 which had also liberated Fairbank, but Hayden realized what the Fugitive Slave Law would mean for his family and friends. Harriet and Joseph were still fugitives and Boston had almost 2,000 blacks, many of them former slaves. Quick action was needed.

A meeting of the "Colored Citizens of Boston" was held on September 30 to respond to the dangers of the Fugitive Slave Law. The overflowing crowd quickly chose Lewis Hayden as chairman. Standing at the podium, Hayden opened the meeting by calling for "the adoption of ways and means for the protection of those in Boston liable to be seized by the prowling man-thief." William Lloyd Garrison was one of the first speakers, and the crowd enthusiastically endorsed his attacks on the Fugitive Slave Law. But black Bostonians had moved beyond Garrison's calls for moral suasion and nonresistance to a more radical stance.

After Garrison the meeting was dominated by speakers of African descent—Josiah Henson (Hayden's friend from Canada), John T. Hilton, and William Nell. With frequent references to Patrick Henry's call for "Liberty or death!" the assembly passed resolutions including a statement that "they who would be free, themselves must strike the blow" and a pledge to "defend ourselves and each other in resisting this God-defying and inhuman law, at any and every sacrifice, invoking Heaven's defence of the right."[3] Before adjourning, the crowd selected a committee of seven men, including Hayden, to plan another meeting.

According to the *Liberator*, the follow-up meeting on October 4 was attended by "a vast concourse, including fugitives and their friends." The first order of business was the election of Lewis Hayden as president. The former slave, who was not deemed a worthy agent of the American Anti-Slavery Society, had become the acknowledged leader of Boston's black community.

Black speakers at the meeting quickly discarded any thoughts of nonresistance. Joshua B. Smith, a successful caterer, urged every fugitive to obtain a revolver and declared, "If liberty is not worth fighting for, it is not worth having."

Robert Johnson asked women working in Boston's hotels to watch for "Southern slave catchers" and to give the alarm. At the same time, he cautioned men that they should not be the aggressors, but if the slave hunter attacks—"kill him."

When his turn came, Garrison admitted he was a nonresistant and, with the help of God, he was determined to live and die as one. In that light, he predicted "the fugitives in this city and elsewhere, would be more indebted to the moral power of public sentiment than to any display of physical resistance." Nonetheless, Garrison was able to introduce a lengthy resolution, with great support from the floor, repeatedly calling on the clergy of Massachusetts to "denounce the law!"

The evening belonged, however, to those threatened by the law and those willing to resist it. Charles Lenox Remond, even though he had never been a slave, pointed out the harsh provisions of the law "made all colored persons fugitives." Remond asked his friends to stay and struggle for freedom rather than flee to Canada. Robert Morris, the first black attorney in Massachusetts, presented ten resolutions prepared by Hayden and the leadership committee. The assembly unanimously approved the resolutions including the hope that "the citizens of Boston will rally in Faneuil Hall, and send forth, in the ear of Christendom, their opinion of the infamous Fugitive Slave Bill."[4]

The "fugitives and their friends" who called for a rally were not disappointed. On October 14, 1850 an immense meeting was held in Faneuil Hall, Boston's historic meeting place near the waterfront sometimes referred to as the "Cradle of Liberty." Hundreds of Bostonians attended. Frederick Douglass and Wendell Phillips, the greatest orators of the anti-slavery movement, were the principal speakers.

Douglass had traveled from Rochester, New York for the meeting and described the panic along his route as many of his brethren made plans to flee to Canada. He pointed out that slaveholders did not want to recapture their slaves for their economic value, for "One who has tasted the sweets of liberty can never again make a profitable slave!" Instead, according to Douglass, slaveowners wished to recapture the fugitives "in order to make examples of them; and the slave knows that, if returned, he will have to submit to excruciating torture."

Wendell Phillips spoke next. Amid great cheers, he called for defiance of the Fugitive Slave Law: "The law expects disobedience, provides for disobedience, and God forbid that it should be disappointed."[5]

Responding to the speeches, the assembly appointed a Committee of Vigilance and Safety with fifty members. In addition to Hayden and Wendell Phillips, the Committee included Francis Jackson, Theodore Parker, Hayden's friend John A. Andrew, and another man who would also become one of Hayden's lifelong friends, Dr. Henry Bowditch. Bostonians of African descent were represented by Hayden, William Nell, Robert Morris, John T. Hilton, and Joshua B. Smith. Nell, Morris, and Hilton were already well known for their ongoing fight to integrate the Boston public schools. Among the names noticeably absent from the membership of the Vigilance Committee, however, was that of William Lloyd Garrison.

Leadership was shared by blacks and whites. Hayden and Smith were appointed to the executive committee with Phillips and Parker. Morris was put on the finance committee with Andrew, Bowditch, and Jackson. The assembly also approved a resolution empowering Committee members "to take all measures which they shall deem expedient to protect the colored people of this city in the enjoyment of their lives and liberties." The Vigilance Committee would not have to wait long for its first challenge.

Declaration of Sentiments
of the
Colored Citizens of Boston
on the
Fugitive Slave Bill

. . . believing that 'Resistance to tyrants is obedience to God' we are now

Resolved, To organize a League of Freedom, composed of all those who are ready to resist the law, rescue and protect the slave, at every hazard, and who remember that
'Whether on the scaffold high,
Or in the battle's van,
The fittest place where *man* can die,
Is where he dies for *man*.'

Resolved, That in view of the imminent danger, present and looked for, we caution every colored man, woman and child, to be careful in their walks through the highways and byways of the city, by day, and doubly so, if out at night, as to *where* they go—*how* they go— and *whom* they go with; to be guarded on side, off side, and all sides; as watchful as Argus with his hundred eyes, and as executive as was Briareus with as many hands; if seized by any one, to make the air resound with the signal-word, and as they would rid themselves of any wild beast, be prompt in their hour of peril.

Resolved, That any Commissioner who would deliver up a fugitive slave to a Southern highwayman, under this infamous and unconstitutional law, would have delivered up Jesus Christ to his prosecutors for one third of the price that Judas Iscariot did.

Resolved, That in the event of any Commissioner of Massachusetts being applied to for remanding a fugitive, we trust he will emulate the example of Judge Harrington of Vermont, and 'be satisfied with nothing short of a bill of sale from the Almighty.'

Resolved, That though we learn that bribes have already been offered to our Judiciary to forestall their influence against the panting fugitive, we would not attempt any offset, than to remind said officers that

'Man is more than Constitutions; better rot beneath the sod, Than be true to Church and State, while we are doubly
    false to God.'

that should he, in the emergency, obey God rather than the devil, by letting the oppressed go free, he will have done his part in wiping out from the escutcheon of Massachusetts the foul stain inflicted by Daniel Webster in promoting and Samuel A. Eliot in voting for, this Heaven-defying law.

Resolved, That though we gratefully acknowledge that the mane of the British Lion affords a nestling-place to our brethren in danger from the claws of the American Eagle, we would, nevertheless, counsel against their leaving the soil of their birth, consecrated by their tears, toils and perils, but yet to be rendered, truly, 'the land of the free and the home of the brave.' The ties of consanguinity bid *all* remain, *who* would lend a helping hand to the millions now in bonds. But at all events, if the soil of Bunker Hill, Concord and Lexington is the last bulwark of liberty, we can nowhere fill more honorable graves.

Resolved, That we do earnestly express the hope that the citizens of Boston will rally in Faneuil Hall, and send forth, in the ear of all Christendom, their opinion of the infamous Fugitive Slave Bill, and of their intent to *dis*obey its decrees. Their voice, uttered in the Cradle of Liberty, will assure us, as nothing else can, whether they are to be reckoned on the side of liberty or slavery—whether they will vouchsafe to us their aid, or will assist the manthief in hurling us and our little ones into bondage.

Resolved, That this meeting would invite the clergymen of this city and vicinity to dedicate a day, or part thereof, to presenting to their people, by prayer and sermon, their Christian duty towards the flying fugitive, and also in acceding to the requisitions of this atrocious Bill.

Resolved, That as in union strength, and in this crisis, a combination of power is all-important, this meeting recommend the calling of a New England Convention of the friends of Liberty to operate against the Fugitive Law, and to devise ways and means for consolidating their resources here on the soil.

Resolved, That the doings of this and the preceding meeting be published for wide circulation.

Resolutions from a meeting held in the Belknap Street Church,
Friday Evening, October 4, 1850
As published in the *Liberator*, October 11, 1850

7. The First Challenge

"Lewis, bolt the door! Quick!"

A week after the meeting at Faneuil Hall, Lewis Hayden was getting ready to lock his clothing store for the day, when William Craft burst in.

"William, what's the matter? You look like a deer in flight."

"I am. Two men from Georgia—John Knight and Willis Hughes—they're here to capture Ellen and me."

Hayden secured the door as his friend scanned the street. "Where did you see them?"

"Knight came into my shop today. Said he was in town on business." Craft fingered a revolver in his belt as he spoke. "He told me Hughes was here too. Then he asked me to go for a walk, show him around."

"Obviously you didn't go."

"No. I was sure Hughes was hiding outside. Hughes is a jailer in Macon—and a slave catcher. They want to take us back." Craft looked toward the door again.

"I locked my door as soon as Knight went out, but I waited to be sure they were gone. Then sneaked out the back."

"We have to get home to warn Ellen and Harriet," said Hayden.

"Then we must get you and Ellen out of Boston, to some place safe."

"I won't go, Lewis. Boston is our home. We've run too far. I won't leave."

"In that case we'll hide Ellen for a few days—some place out of town, but not far. And we'll mobilize the Vigilance Committee. You will be our first challenge."

Lewis Hayden's friends Ellen and William Craft were relatively new to Boston, but they were an important part of Boston's anti-slavery community. The Crafts had arrived in Boston after a remarkable escape from bondage.

William and Ellen had been slaves in Macon, Georgia. Although they had different owners, they were allowed to marry and live together. William's master hired him out as a cabinetmaker. Ellen worked as a seamstress. After seeing children torn from their parents at slave auctions, William and Ellen decided not to have children as long as they were slaves. In the fall of 1848, the young couple made plans to escape from Georgia and from slavery.

By any direct route, the Crafts were over 400 miles from the nearest free state, but secret overland travel through strange areas, where they knew no one, was too risky. Instead, William and Ellen decided to travel to the free states of the eastern seaboard, over the same route as any free white person—south and east by train to Savannah, Georgia and then north to freedom by a combination of steamboat and train.

The couple also decided they would not try to hide themselves—they would only hide their identities. Ellen, who had a light complexion, would disguise herself as a slave-owning gentleman traveling to Philadelphia for medical treatment. William would be "his" loyal slave.

Ellen Craft escaped from slavery with her husband, William, by posing as his white "master." She often appeared at anti-slavery rallies wearing her disguise. By permission of the Houghton Library, Harvard University

Despite her light skin, Ellen had a number of shortcomings if she was to pose as a gentleman: She had the smooth, beardless face of a woman and she could neither read nor write. William and Ellen created a costume to hide her deficiencies. The "slaveowner" would have bandages to conceal a beardless face. Dark glasses would allow the "gentleman" to avoid reading, due to poor eyesight. And a bandaged right arm would allow "him" to avoid signing his name.

Just before Christmas, 1848, Ellen and William gathered the money they had saved, dressed Ellen in her costume, and began their journey.

The fugitive couple traveled openly through the heart of the slave states, first by train to Savannah; then by steamboat to Charleston, South Carolina; and on to Richmond, Virginia. Ellen, dressed as a gentleman, traveled in first-class accommodations and mingled with elite passengers, disguising her voice in low tones. William often rode in the last car of the train with other slaves or slept on the deck of the boat as a part of the cargo.

When the couple reached Baltimore, their last stop in a slave state, the ticket agent sold the "slaveowner" a ticket to Philadelphia. He refused, however, to issue a ticket for the slave without a bond, since the railroad did not want to be liable for slaves escaping over its rails. William pleaded that he was required to help his "master" reach desperately needed medical treatment. Impressed by the plea, a Southern gentleman who had traveled with the feeble "slaveowner" stepped forward and signed a bond for William.

In Philadelphia, William and Ellen made contact with Quakers who fed and clothed them, gave William and Ellen their first reading instructions, and then sent them on to Boston.

The Crafts traveled almost 1,000 miles in their total journey from Macon to Boston, where the abolitionists warmly welcomed the brave couple to their new home. The Crafts were popular figures at anti-slavery rallies because of the dramatic nature of their escape, as well as their abilities as public speakers. Ellen would sometimes stun audiences by appearing in her disguise as a white male slaveowner.

Despite their success, the Crafts soon tired of public speaking and yearned to establish a family life. When William Wells Brown, their speaking partner, left for Europe in May 1849, the Crafts seized the opportunity to settle down and pursue their trades.

Ellen and William Craft's first home in Boston was with Harriet and Lewis Hayden. Ellen earned money as a seamstress. William opened a used furniture store. Although Lewis was ten years older than William, they became close friends and worked together on anti-slavery issues. When Hayden was elected president at the

October 4 meeting to oppose the Fugitive Slave Law, Craft was elected a vice-president.

The story of the Crafts' bold escape had appeared in newspapers throughout the country. William and Ellen's former owners easily discovered the location of their former slaves and sent Hughes and Knight to Boston. When the slave hunters could not capture the fugitives by trickery, they went to federal court and obtained a warrant for the arrest of Ellen and William Craft under the terms of the Fugitive Slave Law.

The Vigilance Committee, now grown to over 100 members, responded with action. Committee members kept constant record of the whereabouts of Hughes and Knight. Placards were posted describing the slave hunters and warning of their presence. Henry Bowditch took Ellen to the home of a friend, just outside Boston.

Hayden and Craft knew that the slave hunters, with their warrant in hand, could call on the forces of the United States government to forcibly arrest William and Ellen, wherever and whenever they could find them. In response, the former slaves converted Hayden's boardinghouse into a fortress. Lewis Hayden, Joseph Hayden, William Craft, and other blacks barricaded themselves in the Hayden home. Heavily armed, with two kegs of gunpowder in his cellar and a lighted torch in his hand, Hayden sent word that he would blow up himself, his house, and any slave hunters or United States marshals who attempted to force their way into his home to arrest William Craft. The attempt was never made.

While Knight and Hughes pursued William and Ellen, the Vigilance Committee pursued the slave hunters. Knight and Hughes were followed and shouted at in the streets. They were slapped with a host of nuisance suits including charges of driving their carriage too fast, smoking in the streets, swearing in the streets, and carrying concealed weapons. They were forced to post a bond of $10,000 for slandering William by saying he had stolen his clothes and his body when he left Georgia, another bond of $10,000 for damage to William's business reputation, and $20,000 more for slandering Ellen. Yet sufficient funds were repeatedly found in Boston to post bail for the slave hunters from Georgia.

Finally Hayden, Theodore Parker and fifty-eight other members of the Vigilance Committee called on Knight and Hughes in their hotel. Parker, a minister, told them he had saved them from violence thus far, but he could not guarantee their continued safety. The slave hunters left Boston on Wednesday afternoon, October 30.

William and Ellen now realized they would never be safe in the United States as long as the Fugitive Slave Law was in effect. Friends urged them to leave for England, where slavery had been banned for almost twenty years, and held a meeting to raise money for the journey. The foremost anti-slavery leaders attended. Garrison, Phillips, and Parker were there, of course. So was Ralph Waldo Emerson. Even Charles Sumner, soon to be the United States senator from Massachusetts, was among the small but elite gathering.

Hayden rose to address the group. Moved by his strong feelings for William and Ellen, he spoke with unusual eloquence. Then, looking at his audience, he was seized by the thought of lecturing the greatest orators of his age and quietly slipped back into his chair. Wendell Phillips, the man who had fired Hayden as an agent of the American Anti-Slavery Society, followed Hayden and each of the noted guests spoke in turn. The donations were generous. The group raised enough money to pay for the Crafts' passage to England and to provide funds for the start of their new life.

Before leaving for England, William and Ellen had one request—they asked to have a wedding ceremony, since as slaves they had never been formally married. On November 7, 1850, the elite of the abolition movement gathered in the parlor of the Hayden boardinghouse to celebrate the marriage of William and Ellen Craft. Among the special guests was Lewis and Harriet's old friend, Calvin Fairbank.

Reverend Theodore Parker performed the service and turned the ceremony into a demonstration against the Fugitive Slave Law. Seeing a Bible and a large Bowie knife on an adjacent table, Parker charged William with defending his wife as well as himself. He then handed William the Bible and the knife—one for defense of the soul, the other for the defense of the body.

The Crafts left for England by way of Nova Scotia. Their trip was marred by bad luck, bad weather, and discrimination, even in Canada, but they arrived safely in England by the middle of December, just two years after leaving Georgia.

The scheme to return the Crafts to slavery was the first of four notable attempts to recapture slaves in Boston under the terms of the Fugitive Slave Law. Each attempt was more dramatic than the one before. And each attempt elicited a stronger response from the Vigilance Committee and from Lewis Hayden.

8. In the Fiery Furnace

Among the fugitives living in Boston in 1851 was a runaway slave named Shadrach. The young man had escaped from Norfolk, Virginia where he was the property of John DeBree, a United States Navy paymaster. After reaching Boston, Shadrach found employment as a waiter at the Cornhill Coffee House. In the Bible, "Shadrach" is the name of one of three young men miraculously delivered by their God from out of a fiery furnace. Ironically, Shadrach would be the first of three young men thrown into Boston's version of the fiery furnace.

DeBree commissioned John Caphart to capture Shadrach. Caphart was a constable in Norfolk and operated a private slave jail, where he offered to whip slaves for fifty cents per flogging. The slave hunter arrived in Boston on Wednesday, February 12, 1851 and by Friday he had a warrant for Shadrach's arrest. On Saturday morning, Deputy United States Marshal Patrick Riley entered the Cornhill Coffee House with the warrant and nine deputies. Riley was not a "neutral" in the matter of escaped slaves. Three months earlier, he had helped arrange bond for Hughes and Knight when they were arrested while pursuing William and Ellen Craft.

Riley and his deputies innocently sat down for coffee in groups of three and four. A number of blacks, both waiters and customers, were in the coffee house. Riley knew Shadrach worked there, but his informant, the man who would identify the runaway slave, was late. Then Riley heard someone address his waiter as "Shadrach"—the very man the marshal was looking for.

Riley asked for his bill and handed the waiter the money. When Shadrach went to the counter for change, Riley and two of his deputies followed. As they neared the back door, the deputies grabbed the former slave and pulled him into the street. Within minutes, Shadrach, still wearing his apron, was dragged into the Suffolk County courthouse.

Federal officials imprisoned Shadrach in a federal courtroom located in the county courthouse. Since an 1843 Massachusetts law prohibited holding accused slaves in county jails, and since there was no federal jail in Boston, the federal courtroom also had to serve as a jail cell. Within an hour, a half-dozen anti-slavery attorneys, including Richard Henry Dana, Ellis Gray Loring, and Robert Morris, were at the courthouse volunteering to defend the prisoner. Meanwhile, Lewis Hayden was gathering members of Boston's black community, bringing them into the courthouse, to the door of the federal courtroom.

In a hastily prepared hearing, Dana succeeded in getting a postponement to prepare Shadrach's defense. Following the hearing, Dana returned to this office, and most of the spectators left the courtroom. By 12:30 P.M., only Marshal Riley with four or five of his deputies; Shadrach with five of his friends, including Morris; and Elizur Wright, a newspaper writer friendly to the anti-slavery cause; remained in the courtroom. Hayden and his friends stood in the hallway outside.

While he waited for Morris to finish meeting with Shadrach, Riley pointed out that Shadrach was for sale and offered to donate $25 to a fund to purchase the slave's freedom. Wright replied that if anyone was to be sold, it should be the fellows who had already sold themselves to the kidnappers.

Riley defended himself saying "he only did what he was obliged to do," but Wright turned Riley's words against him, answering that he "thought no law could oblige a man to assist in such atrocious villainy." Obviously offended, Riley ordered his deputies to clear the courtroom.[1]

As a deputy opened the door for Wright to leave, there was a shout in the hall and the crowd charged against the partially open door. Riley rushed across the room to reinforce his man at the door, while calling for help. In the confusion, Shadrach found himself unguarded and ran for the opposite door, but he was intercepted by a deputy. Still trying to hold the door against the crowd, Riley shouted "Shoot him! Shoot him!" but his deputies lacked either the weapons or the will, and no shots were fired.[2]

The rescue party quickly filled the courtroom, trapping Riley behind the door. Riley's outnumbered deputies offered little resistance. As Hayden and the other liberators passed through the courtroom, they absorbed Shadrach into their number and carried him out of the courthouse, into the street, and back to the black neighborhood. Hayden and Morris hid Shadrach in the attic of an elderly woman, and the rescuers dispersed.

Hayden returned to the hiding place after dark. His first priority was to get the escaped prisoner out of Boston. After freeing Shadrach from the attic, Hayden hired a cab to drive himself and his companion across the Charles River to the home of a friend in Cambridge. Hayden spent Sunday afternoon with Shadrach, then returned to Boston.

Back in Boston, Hayden hired a wagon, large and well suited to hiding a fugitive. Going back to Cambridge, Hayden met Shadrach on Sunday evening and drove him 15 miles to Concord, where they reached the home of Francis Edwin Bigelow at 3:30 Monday morning. In the interest of secrecy, Shadrach and Hayden were taken to the Bigelows' bedroom where breakfast was prepared on a small stove. Years later, Mrs. Bigelow vividly recalled the men eating breakfast at that early hour from plates spread on her bureau. When Hayden returned to Boston, Mr. Bigelow drove Shadrach another 20 miles to the next stop on the Underground Railroad.

The abolitionists were pleased. A fugitive had been rescued quickly and without violence. Even Garrison, the nonresistant, praised the success: "Nobody injured, nobody wronged, but simply a chattel transformed into a man, and conducted to a spot whereon he can glorify God in his body and his spirit, which are his."[3]

Federal officials were furious. President Millard Fillmore directed that "prosecutions be commenced against all persons who shall have made themselves aiders or abettors in this flagitious offense."[4] Henry Clay, the senator from Kentucky and a main architect of the Fugitive Slave Law, was outraged. Speaking on the floor of the Senate he asked:

> By whom was the mob impelled onward? By our own race? No, sir, but by negroes [*sic*]; by African descendants; by people who possess no part, as I contend, in our political system; and the question which arises is, whether we shall have law, and whether the majesty of Government shall be maintained or not; whether we shall have a Government of white men or black men in the cities of his country.[5]

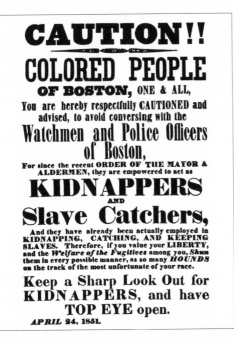

This placard by Theodore Parker warned the black community to beware of the danger they faced even from the police of their own city. Courtesy of the Ontario Black History Society

What would Clay have said had he known that the leader of the mob was the man whose wife he had sold some fifteen years before in Lexington?

The government wasted no time in seeking revenge. Federal marshals quickly seized newspaper correspondent Elizur Wright and attorney Charles G. Davis. Two black men, James Scott and John Foyce, were among four others arrested for their part in the rescue. On February 21, U.S. Marshal Charles Devens, who was out of town when Riley arrested Shadrach, obtained sixty revolvers and distributed them among his men. The next day, Devens arrested Hayden and Morris as the seventh and eighth conspirators. The abolitionists rallied around the accused. James Buffum, a former agent of the American Anti-Slavery Society, posted Hayden's bail of $3,000. A former Boston mayor posted bond for Morris. The Vigilance Committee gathered contributions and hired Richard Henry Dana, John T. Hale, and George Farley as attorneys.

The men indicted for liberating Shadrach were tried separately in June 1851. Federal prosecutors went to great lengths to select jury members who would enforce the Fugitive Slave Law. At the conclusion of Hayden's trial, a majority of the jury were for conviction, but at least one juror held out for "not guilty" and the judge declared a mistrial. Similar results were reached in all the rescue trials and the charges against Hayden and the other defendants were eventually dismissed.

About a year after the trials, Dana learned a secret that shed light on the failure to convict Shadrach's rescue team. After giving a speech in rural Massachusetts, near the New Hampshire state line, Dana was approached by a man he recognized from the trials. The former juror told Dana why, at least in one trial, it was impossible for prosecutors to get a conviction. "I was the twelfth juror in that case, and I was the man who drove Shadrach over the [state] line."[6]

Less than sixty days after Shadrach's escape, the slave hunters struck again. On the night of April 3, 1851, a second Bostonian was arrested and imprisoned in the courthouse. The prisoner was Thomas Sims, a twenty-three-year-old fugitive from Savannah, Georgia. Sims had escaped from slavery by stowing away on a ship bound for Boston.

As with Shadrach, federal marshals were denied use of a jail because of the Massachusetts law forbidding the use of the county jail in slave cases. The marshals had learned a lesson from Shadrach's escape, however, and they imprisoned Sims in a federal jury room on the third floor of the courthouse.

Members of the Vigilance Committee were quickly called to a meeting in the offices of the *Liberator*. Among those present was Thomas Wentworth Higginson, a young minister from just outside Boston, known to his friends as "Wentworth."

The meeting was chaotic. Garrison sat in a corner, ignoring the group and setting type for his next editorial in the *Liberator*. Meanwhile his followers, the nonresistants, suggested prayers and speeches. Higginson called for dramatic action, a rescue of Sims by force. A few of the abolitionists agreed with Higginson's intent, but refused to approve any plan that would violate the rules of "good citizenship."

Frustrated by the Committee's inability to make a decision, Higginson mentioned that the lack of action "would not, however, apply to the negroes, it might well seem; they had just proved their mettle, and would doubtless do it again."

Higginson recorded the response: "On my saying this in the meeting, Lewis Hayden, the leading negro in Boston, nodded cordially and said, 'Of course they will.' Soon after drawing me aside, he startled me adding, 'I said that for a bluff, you know. We do not wish anyone to know how really weak we are. Practically there are no colored men in Boston; the Shadrach prosecutions have scattered them all. What is to be done must be done without them.'" Higginson was stunned, "Here was a blow indeed!" [7]

Because of Shadrach's rescue, federal officials were prepared for an attempt to rescue Sims. But with few blacks to help, the rescuers' numbers were reduced against a wiser and larger federal force. Despite the fact that Hayden was still under indictment for his role in Shadrach's escape (his trial had not yet occurred), he agreed to join a half dozen men, including Higginson and Henry Bowditch, who were committed to action.

Also willing to act was Hayden's pastor, the Reverend Leonard Grimes from the Twelfth Baptist Church, which was often known as the "fugitive slave church."[8] Grimes was well aware of the reduced strength of Boston's black community—sixty members of his congregation had fled Boston since Shadrach's arrest—but Grimes had a special role to play. As a minister and as a leading member of Boston's black community, he was the only person federal officials allowed to visit the imprisoned Sims.

Hayden, Higginson, Bowditch, Grimes, and the others reviewed the preparations officials had made to hold a single prisoner. Over 100 armed men—United States marshals, city policemen, and state militia men—guarded the courthouse. Heavy chains stretched across every entry to prevent a rush such as had saved Shadrach. Elizur Wright's newspaper, the *Commonwealth*, reported that the chains around the courthouse bound it "to the Georgia cotton presses." Other abolitionists pointed out that state officials, bowing under the chains as they entered the courthouse, were living symbols of the government's submission to the slave powers.

The rescue committee devised a desperate plan. The third floor room where Sims was held had a window overlooking the courthouse square. According to the plan, Hayden, Higginson, and Bowditch would gather mattresses in the offices of sympathetic attorneys around the square, possibly the offices of Dana and Morris. At a specified time, the mattresses would be rushed to a spot below the window. Sims would jump through the window onto the mattresses. A carriage would race into the square (probably driven by Hayden as he had done for Shadrach) and Sims would be conveyed to the Underground Railroad. Grimes was assigned to deliver the plan to the prisoner.

All was made ready. The mattresses were obtained and hidden in the offices. The carriage was reserved. The message was delivered.

When Hayden and Higginson visited the court square at dusk on the appointed day, they were astonished to see workmen installing iron bars on the windows of Sims's room. Their plan was impossible. The rescue attempt was defeated.

Sims's case was heard by George Curtis, U.S. Circuit Court Commissioner. Despite a flurry of legal activity on Sims's behalf, Curtis ruled that Sims was a slave and ordered him returned to his master. Curtis apologized for doing his duty and announced he would not accept the $10 fee.

In the predawn hours of April 12, 1851, 100 armed volunteers formed a hollow square in front of the Boston courthouse. Approximately the same number of city police formed a double row to the courthouse door. At 4:30 A.M., Sims was led out, tears running down his cheeks. The human fortress surrounded him and escorted him through the streets to Boston Harbor where a ship waited to return Sims to slavery.

According to Henry Bowditch, he and his son were among the abolitionists lining the streets calling "Shame!" and "Infamy!" as the procession passed. At the site of the Boston Massacre, where Crispus Attucks, a sailor of mixed race, had been among the first to die in the prelude to the American Revolution, Bowditch and his friends angrily "pointed out to those minions of slavery the holy spot over which they were treading."[9]

Bowditch did not name Hayden and Higginson as being among those calling from the sidewalks when Sims passed by. Useless name-calling was not their style. Hayden and Higginson had resolved that the next time a fugitive slave was seized in Boston, they would be ready.

9. "THE TEMPLE OF REFUGE"

Despite his arrest in the Shadrach case and the government's show of force in the Sims case, Lewis Hayden and the members of the Vigilance Committee continued to defy the Fugitive Slave Law by assisting the escaped slaves who reached Boston.

In September of 1851, only five months after Thomas Sims was marched out of Boston, James Freeman Clarke, a prominent Boston minister, wrote a friend about his delight at seeing Theodore Parker and "some six or eight colored people, including Lewis Hayden" among his congregation that Sunday. The minister pointed out with pride that "Parker, Hayden, [Robert] Walcutt, Dr. [Henry] Bowditch, and [Henry] Prentiss were called out just after the sermon began, to attend to a slave mother and child just arrived in a vessel from Virginia."[1]

In another instance, a group from the Vigilance Committee, including Wendell Phillips and Austin Bearse, who was captain of a small coastal boat often used by the abolitionists, went to the Boston wharf on a tip that a slave was being held on a boat recently arrived from the South. The slave had tried to escape as a stowaway but had been caught, and was imprisoned on shipboard awaiting the return trip south.

Phillips and Bearse searched the vessel in question and another boat of the same owner. They found the former stowaway on the second boat, escorted him out of the harbor, and put him into a carriage headed for the Hayden boardinghouse.

This fugitive lived with the Haydens for about two weeks, until Lewis reported to the Vigilance Committee that his house was closely watched by a constable and by policemen. Hayden felt his visitor should be removed at once.

Apparently someone recalled that Ellen Craft had escaped from slavery dressed as a young man, and the Committee agreed to reverse the process, disguising their male fugitive as a woman. William Bowditch, Henry's brother, drove his carriage to the Hayden house. When Bowditch opened the carriage door a "woman" came out Hayden's front door and climbed into the coach. Within a few hours Bowditch's passenger was in Concord, on his way to Canada.

Lewis Hayden did not operate the boardinghouse at 66 Southac Street alone. While there are few references in existing documents to Harriet Hayden, she must have worked with Lewis, feeding and sheltering fugitives in their home and distributing clothing to former slaves headed north.

If the Haydens kept a guest register for their boardinghouse, it has not survived. Many of their illegal guests are, however, recorded in a journal maintained by Francis Jackson, treasurer of the Boston Vigilance Committee. Jackson carefully entered the names of donors to the Committee, with the amounts of their gifts, as well as the expenses of the Committee on behalf of the fugitives. From November 1850 until August 1857, the Hayden name appears thirty-seven times in the expense column of Jackson's book. The entries indicate Lewis and Harriet were reimbursed for assisting at least 100 fugitives.

The Legal Committee of Vigilance Dr

Explanatory

On the 15th. Feb. 1851 Shadrach, a fugitive Slave from Virginia was arrested at the instance of John Caphart, a slave hunter from Norfolk Va. and taken before Commission Curtis, who after the adjournment of the first examination, was rescued from the Suffolk Court house, by the colored people, & sent to Canada.; For this brave act, Lewis Hayden Robert Morris, James Scott, & Elizur Wright, were arrested, & tried before Judge Sprague of the U.S. Court. & were all acquitted; the expenses of these trials, are herewith recorded, & were defrayed by donations & contributions, entered on the opposite pages of this book.

Hon. John P. Hale, Richard H Dana & Geo. Farley were the Lawyers employed to defend the rescuers.

1851							
May	21	Nath'l Colver for services in collecting money				11	50
"	24	Wm C Nell do do in Salem				15	-
"	"	Nath'l Colver do do				14	
						40	50
		Amount. carried over					

Treasurer Francis Jackson carefully recorded the expenses incurred by the Vigilance Committee in defending Hayden and others accused in the rescue of Shadrach in 1851. By permission of the Bostonian Society, Old State House

"Dec 5 [1851] Lewis Hayden boarding Pews & Hall Fugitives two Weeks $10," was a typical entry. A few months later the Haydens received $51 for boarding "McCooley and daughter," in addition to $12 McCooley had paid from his own funds. Jackson kept exact records for each transaction. For example, in December of 1852 he entered "Lewis Hayden for Jn Wesley $4.38, J. W. Fisher $4.23, Mrs. Smith $2, Tho^S Jackson $2.50 [total] $13.11."

The Haydens were also reimbursed for services that did not include boarding, such as "Clothing to Mrs. H. Fischer etc. $13," "furniture for Jane Wilson & children $15.12," or "Taylor & Coopers fare to Canada $20.50." Perhaps the saddest entry was on October 9, 1853: "Lewis Hayden for Julia Smith funeral of her child $20."

Harriet and Lewis Hayden were not alone in receiving payment for boarding fugitives or for being reimbursed for other good works. Jackson's ledger documents that the Vigilance Committee paid over $4,000 to more than two dozen individuals, including Theodore Parker, for efforts and expenses on behalf of fugitives in Boston. In addition, Jackson recorded the payment of $1,500 to attorneys for the defense of Hayden, Morris, and the others indicted for rescuing Shadrach. Fortunately, Jackson's detailed, secret account of the Vigilance Committee's activities never reached the hands of federal prosecutors. Its contents could have been used to convict the Haydens and a hundred other Bostonians of violations of the Fugitive Slave Law.

Eventually the Haydens connected a tunnel to the subbasement of their boardinghouse. This secret passage was barely large enough to permit one person to crawl through, but in times of danger it allowed fugitives to travel several hundred yards undetected to another home in the area. In this rare instance, the "Underground Railroad" was truly underground.

Henry Bowditch regarded the Hayden home as the "Temple of Refuge."[2] Bowditch had a personal knowledge of the Hayden store and the Hayden boardinghouse because he was one of the many anti-slavery leaders who regularly gathered in those locations for strategy meetings. Black leaders such as Charles Lenox Remond, Leonard Grimes, Robert Morris, Joshua Smith, and John Hilton and white leaders such as Bowditch, Francis Jackson, Wendell Phillips, and Theodore Parker could often be found at one location or the other. A generation later, the *Boston Globe* described Lewis's store: "Here conferences were held and from here rescue parties were sent out."[3]

Among the visitors to the Hayden boardinghouse was Harriet Beecher Stowe, author of *Uncle Tom's Cabin*. Stowe's book, an instant bestseller in 1852, had electrified the nation. Using experiences she had gained while living in Cincinnati, Ohio, and while visiting northern Kentucky, Stowe portrayed slavery as a struggle between slaveowners and slaves, where even the slaves of well-meaning owners were subject to brutality and dehumanizing treatment.

Amid challenges from angry Southerners that she prove her accusations, Stowe resolved to write another book that would describe her personal experiences along the Kentucky-Ohio border and would include first-hand reports from former slaves and from Southerners opposed to slavery.

As part of her research, Stowe visited Boston and the offices of the *Liberator*, asking to be introduced to former slaves. Austin Bearse and Robert Walcutt guided Stowe to the Hayden boardinghouse, where she met Lewis and Harriet as well as the thirteen fugitives they were harboring.

Lewis Hayden and Harriet Stowe had a great deal to talk about.

During her visits to Kentucky, Stowe had witnessed a slave auction near Maysville, the Haydens' last stop in a slave state. Stowe had also visited John Rankin and other stationmasters of the Underground Railroad at Ripley, Ohio, the Haydens' first stop in a free state.

Hayden told the author that when he read in *Uncle Tom's Cabin* about Cassy (a slave who kills her son to save him from slavery), he thought of his mother's attempt on his own life. Stowe's critics claimed no mother would kill a child in order to save him from slavery. In 1853, a few months after her visit with Lewis Hayden, Stowe answered her critics by including the story of Millie Hayden's attack on her son in *The Key to Uncle Tom's Cabin.*

10. "RESCUE HIM!"

After Thomas Sims was returned to slavery, an uneasy peace existed between the authorities and the abolitionists. On May 24, 1854, the peace was broken: That evening United States marshals arrested Anthony Burns, a fugitive slave from Virginia and the third man to be thrown into Boston's version of the "fiery furnace." Marshals imprisoned Burns in the same courthouse where they had held Shadrach and Sims.

Responding to Burns's arrest, sixty members of the Vigilance Committee met the following day and issued a call for a mass meeting in Faneuil Hall the next evening. The Committee chose Wendell Phillips and Theodore Parker as the principal speakers for the event, but other than planning the rally, the Committee was unable to ratify a course of action.

Despite the Committee's indecisiveness, Wentworth Higginson was able to identify a small group of individuals "willing to act forcibly in personal resistance."[1] The activist group chose six members as their leaders. At Higginson's suggestion, Martin Stowell, who had led a slave rescue in Syracuse, was added to the committee. The leaders agreed to meet at Faneuil Hall just before the rally.

Late Friday afternoon, Higginson went to the train station to welcome Stowell. As the pair walked from the station toward the meeting, Stowell analyzed the situation and suggested a plan that struck Higginson as an inspiration. In accordance with Stowell's plan, Higginson stopped in a hardware store, made some purchases that he delivered to friends in the courthouse square, and then headed for the meeting.

When Higginson and Stowell reached Faneuil Hall an enormous crowd was already scrambling to get inside. The pair pushed their way to a small room off the stairway to the main auditorium, but the chaos made it impossible for the committee to meet as planned. As the noisy throng rushed past, Higginson and Stowell tried to describe their strategy to individual leaders.

Higginson explained that the authorities might expect an attack on the courthouse *after* the meeting, but they could be caught off guard *during* the meeting. According to the plan, an advance group would be sent to the courthouse square, where they would arm themselves with the axes Higginson had secretly purchased and hidden earlier that evening.

The leaders strained to hear Higginson over the pandemonium on the stairway. When the advance group was ready, he continued, it would send a messenger to Faneuil Hall to announce that "a mob of negroes [is] already attacking the Court-House!"[2] The speakers would then dismiss the meeting and the audience would rush to the courthouse square. With reinforcements approaching, the advance group would charge the courthouse doors and rescue Burns.

One by one, the activists agreed to the plan, but Higginson found it almost impossible to communicate the details in the midst of the excited crowd. Even the platform speakers were confused. Parker consented, but never fully understood the plan. Higginson

Thomas Wentworth Higginson in 1900, fifty years after he, Lewis Hayden, and others had tried to save fugitive slaves in Boston. Visible is the scar on his chin, split open in the fight to rescue Anthony Burns from slave hunters in 1854. From In After Days: Thoughts on the Future Life, 1910. Courtesy of Archives and Special Collections, University of Kentucky Libraries

never made contact with Phillips, who thought the attack was scheduled for the next day.

Despite the chaos, Higginson readied the advance team. Years later he recalled that the team needed "a nucleus of picked men to head the attack. Stowell, [William] Kemp, and I were each to furnish five of these and Lewis Hayden, the colored leader, agreed to supply ten negroes."[3]

As the public meeting got underway, Hayden, Higginson, and the other members of the advance team separated and walked to the courthouse individually, in order to avoid suspicion. Inside Faneuil Hall, Parker and Phillips were on stage arousing the audience, accusing the men of Boston of being "vassals of Virginia," and thundering, "There is no North . . . the South goes clear to the Canada line." When the attack on the courthouse was announced, the enraged throng bolted for the doors.

At the courthouse, the attack was already underway. One of Hayden's men climbed a lamppost and extinguished a streetlight. Courthouse bells rang, calling out the night watch. Rocks crashed through courthouse windows. Inside, officers shouted orders, sending guards to every door. A pistol was fired from a third-floor window.

The Faneuil Hall crowd rushed into the square. Higginson searched the running figures for the faces of his friends but realized that the desperate attack was the victim of the successful meeting. In the rush to leave the hall, the speakers seated on the platform were cut off from the rear exits by their overflowing audience. Hundreds of men filled the square, but the Faneuil Hall leaders were left behind. According to Higginson, the crowd was dominated by "the froth and scum of the meeting, the fringe of idlers on its edge."[4]

On the west side of the courthouse, Hayden and some of his men found a wooden beam to use as a battering ram. As the group lifted the beam to attack the doorway, Higginson and Stowell came running around the corner and took up their positions. On one side, "a stout negro" held the front of the timber, with Hayden right behind.[5] Higginson took the first position on the other side. Stowell grabbed on across from Hayden. More men lined up on each side. Unknown to Higginson, Hayden and Stowell were armed with pistols.

Amid shouts of "Rescue him! Rescue him!" and "Bring him out!" the team began their attack. The beam crashed against the door. They backed up and charged again, smashing the door open. The first person inside, according to Higginson, was his "black ally." Higginson followed, but before Hayden could enter the guards recovered and closed the door.

Higginson and his ally, stranded inside, were beaten with clubs. Higginson's chin was split open, creating a scar he would carry for the rest of his life. Suddenly, one of the guards, James Batchelder, dropped to the ground, mortally wounded. Neither side had expected death. As the guards removed Batchelder, Higginson and the other attacker slipped out the door.

In the melee after Batchelder's collapse, Hayden fired his pistol, perhaps in an attempt to cover Higginson's retreat. The shot narrowly missed U.S. Marshal Watson Freeman. Later, when Parker heard about the shot he remarked, "Why did he not hit him?"[6]

Standing outside the courthouse with his chin bleeding, Higginson yelled at the crowd of bystanders, "You cowards, will you desert us now?" But no supporters came forward.[7] Lacking reinforcements, with federal troops already approaching, and with the violence having reached an unexpected level, the would-be rescuers withdrew.

The mayor immediately called out two companies of local artillery to guard the courthouse and restore order. For his part, Marshal Freeman summoned two companies from Fort Independence and fifty marines from the Charlestown Navy Yard. By Saturday morning, federal troops and local militia had turned the courthouse square into an armed camp.

Legal challenges by Richard Henry Dana and Charles Ellis on Burns's behalf were useless. On Friday morning, June 2, one week after the attack on the courthouse, Commissioner Edward G. Loring rendered his decision: Burns would be returned to slavery. By 2:30 that afternoon, the forces guarding the courthouse were organized to escort Burns to the wharf.

The parade was led by a detachment of mounted lancers assigned to clear the streets ahead of the procession. A company of United States Marines formed a forward guard. Following the

Anthony Burns, a tall figure in a top hat, being led down Boston's State Street to the docks for return to the South. From *Anthony Burns: A History, 1856.* Courtesy of Lexington Theological Seminary

marines was a hollow square composed of 125 ruffians and street toughs deputized for the occasion. The *Liberator* printed a report describing these men as "the dregs of society; nearly all were blacklegs and thieves."[8] At the center of the hollow square was Marshal Freeman with his prisoner, Anthony Burns. Following Burns and his guards was the Fourth Regiment United States Artillery, with a field cannon. At the rear marched another company of marines.

By some estimates, fifty thousand Bostonians lined the sidewalks to hiss and yell, "Shame!" The hostile crowd flowed into the streets and only retreated to the sidewalks when forced back by mounted lancers. Despite the crowd's outrage, at 3:20 P.M. a steamer departed from the wharf with Burns and many of the marines on board ferrying the prisoner to a federal ship which would take him back to Virginia and slavery.

Also on board the small government ship were Burns's owner and a reporter for the *Boston Herald*. The reporter found Burns "much depressed in mind", but he "seemed considerably elated when the excitement in the city was alluded to, and said, 'There was lots of folks to see a colored man walk through the streets.'"[9]

Burns was gone, but the matter was not over. Upstanding Bostonians were appalled by the chaos in their midst. The *Boston Journal* demanded punishment for the rioters, saying "if lawless violence is to go unrebuked, and men in high social position are to become leaders of a mob . . . Boston will be degraded in the estimation of the whole union."[10]

Stowell and eight other men, four of them of African descent, had been arrested during the courthouse attack. Within twenty-four hours the number arrested had grown to seventeen. When federal marshals arrived at the offices of the *Liberator* with a warrant for the arrest of Lewis Hayden, Hayden was in a back office, talking to a woman who had escaped from slavery with her daughter. Rather than allow federal officers to search the building and possibly capture the fugitives, Hayden stepped to the outer office, announcing, "Here I am. Take me along with you."[11] Eventually Higginson, Parker, and Phillips were added to the list of those arrested for being "riotously and routously engaged."[12]

One month after Burns's return to slavery, the abolitionists celebrated the Fourth of July with a large picnic at Framingham, about fifteen miles west of Boston. Among the speakers was Henry David Thoreau, from Concord. Like Higginson, Thoreau was a

Harvard graduate. Five years before the attack on the Boston courthouse, Thoreau had published his essay, "On the Duty of Civil Disobedience." Higginson and many of the other abolitionists had probably read "Civil Disobedience" with its radical thesis. In the famous essay, Thoreau had written, "Under a government which imprisons any unjustly, the true place for a just man is also a prison."

At the Framingham picnic, Thoreau spoke from notes he had made during the week between the attack on the courthouse and Burns's return to slavery.

> Again it happens that the Boston Court-House is full of armed men, holding a prisoner and trying a MAN, to find out if he is not really a SLAVE . . .
>
> The law will never make men free; it is men who have got to make the law free. They are the lovers of law and order who observe the law when the government breaks it. . . .
>
> Covered with disgrace, the State has sat down coolly to try for their lives and liberties the men who attempted to do its duty for it. And this is called *justice*! They who have shown that they can behave particularly well may perchance be put under bonds for *their good behavior*. They whom truth requires at present to plead guilty are, of all the inhabitants of the State, preeminently innocent. While the Governor, and the Mayor, and countless officers of the Commonwealth are at large, the champions of liberty are imprisoned.
>
> Only they are guiltless who commit the crime of contempt of such a court. It behooves every man to see that his influence is on the side of justice, and let the courts

make their own characters. My sympathies in this case
are wholly with the accused, and wholly against the ac-
cusers and their judges.[13]

Officials were reluctant to prosecute the conspirators. Apparently
one riot was enough. In April 1855 the charges against all conspirators were dismissed on technical grounds.

The question of who killed Batchelder was never resolved. Nor
was it determined conclusively whether he had been stabbed or
shot. Hayden and Higginson never discussed the issue since each
thought the other might have been the killer. Much later, in 1888,
Higginson received evidence that Stowell had shot Batchelder by
firing through the door or through the narrow opening. This theory
may have been correct, but it was also convenient, since Stowell
had died in the Civil War and was unable to defend himself.
Higginson's final speculation was that, in the confusion,
Batchelder was stabbed by some forever unknown assailant, possibly even by one of his own men.

Lewis Hayden and the members of the Vigilance Committee suc-
ceeded in rescuing only one of the three fugitives thrown into
Boston's fiery furnace. The Committee had liberated Shadrach
without violence, but had lost Sims without a struggle, and was de-
feated in the battle for Burns. Despite the failure to rescue Sims and
Burns, the Committee won an important victory over the Fugitive
Slave Law. After the riotous attempt to rescue Anthony Burns in
May 1854, no fugitive slave was ever captured in Boston.

11. "MEN OF ACTION"

One evening in March 1858, Lewis Hayden knocked on the front door of Theodore Parker's home. As Hayden waited for an answer, he wondered why Parker had summoned him this time. Was another rescue in store? Did the unpredictable minister have more "packages" for the Underground Railroad?

Parker opened the door saying only, "Come in." Then he led his guest up three flights of stairs to the large room that was his study. Hayden paused before entering. The sight always amazed him. From Hayden's feet to the far side of the room, thousands of books gathered in living mounds that rose from the floor, to the desk, to the shelves. In a clearing near the window, a bronze statue of Spartacus, the rebellious Roman slave, stood guard on a ledge.

As Hayden picked his way through the books, a young man rose from a sofa to meet him. The stranger was over six feet tall, white, and in his mid-twenties. His smooth hands and fashionable clothes were the marks of a country gentleman, or possibly a college professor with family money.

Parker introduced his guest.

"Lewis, this is Franklin Sanborn. He's a teacher in Concord and a friend of Ralph Emerson."

Hayden stuck out a hand. "I'm pleased to meet you."

"You have many admirers in Concord, Mr. Hayden."

Another guest stood in a far corner, admiring some of the books. The man was older than Hayden, his features were strong and weathered. His lined face was dramatically framed by a long beard reaching down and by hair sweeping up and back. His clothes were warm but out-of-date, the type of clothes a country deacon might wear for a visit to the city.

"Lewis, this is Captain John Brown from New York State, and most recently from Kansas."

"Welcome to Boston, sir. We're honored by your visit."

Brown spoke confidently. "The honor is mine, Mr. Hayden. You and Reverend Parker have risked life and limb for our cause."

Hayden had read in the newspapers about John Brown. For three years, Brown had campaigned in Kansas Territory with his sons to help free-state settlers defeat pro-slavery settlers from the neighboring slave state of Missouri. Brown and his allies hoped to bring Kansas into the Union as a free state.

In the stories from Kansas, Hayden had also read about five pro-slavery men, pulled from their cabins one night in the spring of 1856 and brutally murdered. According to some reports, Brown and his sons committed those murders, but if Brown was willing to fight against slavery, Hayden, like most abolitionists, did not spend a lot of time trying to sort out what might have happened in Kansas two years earlier.

The men sat down and Parker began the meeting.

"We have rescued a few slaves, Lewis, and we have sent fugitives on to Canada, but there are still four million waiting to be free. We've not done much for them."

"Lewis, Captain Brown has a plan to bring an end to slavery."

Hayden turned to Brown, "What is your plan?"

John Brown.

By permission, The Kansas State
Historical Society, Topeka, Kansas

The older man leaned forward, "For reasons of secrecy, I can-
not be specific. But I intend to incite a rebellion in a slave state."
As Brown spoke, he lost the look of a country deacon and took on
the demeanor of a military commander. "I will release slaves and
I will get slaves to join my army. Hearing of our attack, other
slaves will rebel and our revolt will sweep across the South."

"That's a dangerous plan, Mr. Brown," remarked Hayden.

"The rewards will be great. For myself, I expect nothing but to
endure hardness; but I expect to effect a mighty conquest, even
though it be like the last victory of Samson."[1]

Hayden turned to Parker. "This is not a matter for our friends
advocating 'moral suasion.' I don't think Mr. Garrison or your
neighbor, Mr. Phillips, will approve."

"I agree," interrupted Brown. "Men who have the gift of elo-

quence, such as our friend Phillips, seldom are men of action. It is men of action I wish to consult. You need say nothing to Wendell Phillips."[2]

"You're right, of course," said Parker, putting a hand on Brown's shoulder, "but we have friends who are men of action."

Parker was excited. "We've formed a committee, Lewis. Wentworth Higginson is one of us. We also have Gerrit Smith, in New York."

Hayden nodded, "I know Higginson well. I've known Smith since the first conventions I attended. He's a former congress-man—very wealthy—and very generous."

"We also have Dr. Samuel Howe, from here in Boston, and we have George Luther Stearns."

"Howe is a member of our Vigilance Committee and is well known for his work with the blind," replied Hayden. "What about Stearns?"

"He's a manufacturer from Medford, quite successful." Unable to contain his enthusiasm, Parker walked to the front of his desk. Beyond him Hayden could see a musket hanging on the wall—the musket Parker's grandfather had carried in defiance of the British at Lexington Common.

"There's six of us willing to help Captain Brown," Parker con-tinued. "With you we'd have seven. Sanborn has agreed to be sec-retary, keeping us in communication."

"What do you need?" asked Hayden.

"Captain Brown needs money, weapons, and men." Sanborn spoke for the first time. "As for money, Smith and Stearns are well-to-do and have given generously. The rest of us give what we can."

Parker jumped in from across the room, "Stearns and Higginson have arranged for Brown to have rifles that were stockpiled for use in Kansas, but are no longer needed there."

"What do you want from me?"

Parker spoke first. "Lewis, the attack will come this summer and when the time comes we'll need men. Negro men."

"Frederick Douglass and I have been friends for many years," boasted Brown, "I am sure he will help. I also hope to enlist Harriet Tubman and her friends along the Canadian border."

"If you already have Douglass and you plan to recruit Tubman, why do you need me?" asked Lewis. "'Too many cooks can spoil the broth,' Captain Brown, especially when secret plans are involved."

Parker returned to his chair. "Captain Brown doesn't agree, Lewis, but we can't count on Douglass or Tubman. Douglass is a newspaper editor, not a man of action. Tubman believes in action, but her friends are spread across New York and Canada. She has no base of support. We need to find Negroes willing to return to a slave state and fight under Brown. No one can do this as well as you."

Hayden nodded. "If you need me, when the time comes, I will do what I can."

Parker uttered an emphatic, "Thank you, Lewis. Thank you." Brown and Sanborn replied with a nod.

Hayden rose to leave, then addressed the older man. "Captain Brown, my wife and I operate a good boardinghouse. When you return to Boston, please be our guest."

Brown shook Hayden's hand. "Thank you, sir. I may do that."

Parker and the others believed an attack would be launched soon, but shortly after visiting Boston, Brown learned that a former member of his band had turned against him. Fearing disclosure of his plans, Brown delayed his attack.

In May 1859, Brown returned to New England. He spent May 9,

his fifty-ninth birthday, with Sanborn in Concord. Then Sanborn escorted him to Boston for more meetings. During Brown's three-week stay in Boston, his secret committee gave him $2,000.

In July, Brown moved into slave territory with a handful of men and rented a farm near Hagerstown, Maryland, four miles from the United States arsenal at Harper's Ferry, Virginia. Since Maryland and Virginia were slave states, Brown kept a man stationed 25 miles north in Chambersburg, Pennsylvania as a link to supporters in the free states. Once he had established his camp, Brown sent his son John, Jr. on a swing through northern states to gather cash and recruits from among their friends.

Early in September, Lewis Hayden answered his door. A young man stood there.

"Mr. Hayden. I'm John Brown, Jr. My father suggested I call on you."

"Come in, Mr. Brown. You are welcome."

Brown entered and sat erect in a hard wooden chair. Hayden remembered John Brown as a man of strength and confidence, yet the young man before him was nervous and distraught. After small talk about the weather and respective families, John Brown, Jr. came to the point.

"Mr. Hayden, we are in a difficult situation. My father is now in a slave state. He has plans for an attack in Virginia. Before he can attack, he needs more money and more men, but I have done a poor job of gathering either one."

"Won't Sanborn and the others help you?" asked Hayden.

"I went to Concord to see Sanborn, but he is out of town. Higginson is angry that my father did not attack last year and will not help. Stearns says he is with us 'no matter what the outcome,' but he refuses to give any more money. Reverend Parker is in Europe."

"What about Douglass and Tubman?"

"I convinced Douglass to meet my father in Pennsylvania. I even gave him money for the trip, but he refuses to help. He thinks the plan will fail. I cannot find Tubman. I went to her home in New York, but she was not there."

"What is your father's plan? How many slaves will he free?"

"I cannot tell you the plan. I don't know all of it myself. I can tell you this: He has 200 rifles originally intended for Kansas. He has 1,000 pikes made from Bowie knives. He has 200 pistols purchased with money from his New England committee."

"Enough weapons for an army of slaves," thought Hayden.

Brown continued, "Of the $2,000 my father received last May, less than $200 remains. Now he has written me saying he needs another $200 or $300. Shipping the arms was expensive and we lack the money to buy ammunition for the rifles and pistols. In addition, my father is supporting a dozen men while they wait for the money and the men I am to recruit."

Brown put his face in his hands. "Mr. Hayden, during the troubles in Kansas, I had an attack of insanity. I could not control myself. I am almost at that point again. I cannot let my father down. We have already lost Higginson and Douglass, and if we do not attack this year, more of our friends will desert us."

Hayden could not help thinking that the desperate young man looked like a boy who had been given too much wood to carry.

"Mr. Brown, your father deserves our help. I will try to get the money and the men he needs."

Lewis Hayden went to work on behalf of John Brown. Hayden knew Tubman was with friends in New Bedford, where the Haydens had lived a dozen years before. He wrote to Tubman asking for her help. He also wrote to Gerrit Smith asking for funds to support Tubman's parents while she campaigned with Brown. On September 16, Hayden wrote to John, Jr.:

> I have sent a note to Harriet, requesting her to come to Boston, saying to her in the note that she must come right on as soon as she received the note which I think she will do, and when she does come I think we will find some way to send her on. I have seen our friend at Concord; he is a true man. I have not yet said anything to anybody except him. I do not think it wise for me to do so. I shall therefore, when Harriet comes, send for our Concord friend, who will attend to the matter. Have you all the hands you wish? Write soon.
>
> Yours, L. H.[3]

"Our friend at Concord" was Sanborn, still a "true man" even though he was absent during John, Jr.'s visit to Boston. Hayden planned to send for Sanborn when Tubman arrived because he was one of the few people, perhaps the only person, who knew how to reach John Brown directly, rather than through John, Jr.

On September 21, John, Jr. hand-copied Hayden's letter and sent the copy, together with other letters he had received and his own reports, to his father. At that point, his fund-raising efforts were so unsuccessful he was forced to ask his father for money. The younger Brown had to admit that "Unless I have something to subsist upon, I cannot devote my whole time to this work, as it is my wish to do so."[4]

Despite Hayden's request, Harriet Tubman did not return to Boston and never traveled to Harper's Ferry. Tubman remained in

New Bedford, suffering from the recurring illnesses that were a legacy of the hardships she had endured as a slave. Unable to deliver Tubman, Hayden searched for recruits and money. By early October, he had recruited half a dozen men willing to join Brown, but they needed money for their families and for traveling expenses. In addition, he still had not raised the money Brown needed for ammunition and supplies.

On a brisk October morning, Hayden was headed for the post office when he saw a young man he knew well—Francis Jackson Merriam. Only twenty-one years old, Merriam was the grandson of Hayden's friend Francis Jackson, the treasurer for a number of anti-slavery organizations and the purse holder for the $650 Hayden raised in 1849 to ransom Calvin Fairbank.

Francis Merriam had inherited his grandfather's hatred of slavery but lacked his grandfather's ability. The young man had only one good eye and may have been mentally unstable, but he was well traveled and well educated, and Hayden knew Merriam had what Brown needed—money.

Hayden was still looking for the $300 Brown had requested, plus additional funds for Brown and for the men Hayden had recruited in Boston. He attracted the young man's attention and after a few words got right to the point.

"I want $500 and must have it."

Hayden was relieved to hear Merriam's answer. "If you have a good cause, you shall have it."[5]

12. JOHN BROWN'S ARMY

Standing on the street corner that October morning, Lewis Hayden explained to Francis Merriam that he needed the $500 to help John Brown in his fight against slavery.

Hayden had found the right man. Merriam revealed he had gone to Kansas in the winter of 1857–58, looking for Brown and hoping to join his band but with no success. When he returned to Boston, Merriam wrote Brown a letter volunteering his services. Merriam had even offered to "acquire the use of the proper tools."[1] In the context of slave liberation, "tools" equaled firearms. Despite a lack of response from Brown, the young man was still ready to serve.

Hayden explained that Brown was already in Chambersburg, Pennsylvania or could be contacted from there. Merriam pledged the funds Brown needed, but he placed a condition on his support. Referring to Brown's location in or near a slave state, Merriam offered, "If you tell me John Brown is there, you can have my money and me along with it."[2] Hayden invited the young radical to his home that evening. He also summoned George Stearns, a member of Brown's secret committee.

As they examined the young man, Hayden and Stearns had

doubts. They were caught between Merriam's physical and mental limitations, and his financial resources. Throughout the night, Hayden and Stearns questioned Merriam about his motives for joining Brown. Finally, as the first rays of morning sun reached the windows, Hayden and Stearns agreed to send Merriam to Franklin Sanborn for his approval.

That afternoon Merriam traveled to Concord, where he spent the evening with Sanborn. Sanborn realized—as John Brown's son Owen would later say—"the only thing very positive about Merriam was his hatred of slavery."[3] But Sanborn also knew Merriam had an inheritance and the young schoolteacher was tired of begging Stearns, Smith, and the others for money—money that was harder to obtain each time Brown delayed his attack. With Sanborn's reluctant blessing, and possibly with his instructions for finding Brown, Merriam returned to Boston on the morning of October 6.

Realizing the importance of Merriam's money, Sanborn wrote a coded but optimistic letter to Wentworth Higginson, hoping to rekindle Higginson's enthusiasm for the project: "Tomorrow or the next day, a Mr. Merriam of Boston . . . will start for the pastures where our shepherd is. He invests some money in the specula- tion . . . The $300 desired has been made up and rec'd."[4]

Back in Boston, Merriam put his affairs in order and gathered $600 in gold. Before heading south, he deposited some of the money with Hayden for the expenses of the black recruits who were to follow. At least one of these men, John Anderson, agreed to follow Merriam in a day or two. As a wealthy gentleman, Merriam could travel by first class train from Boston to Chambersburg, and on to Hagerstown, Maryland. As a black man, Anderson would have to get off the train at Chambersburg, the last stop in a free state. From there he would have to make his way in secret to

Brown's farm, past slave hunters patrolling the Pennsylvania-Maryland border.

Merriam reached Chambersburg on October 9 and made contact with John Brown the next day. Brown did not send the new recruit to his headquarters at the rented farm, but to Philadelphia and then to Baltimore, where Merriam used his money to buy ammunition and supplies for the raid. On Saturday, October 15, Merriam sent Hayden a telegram from Harper's Ferry:

> Orders disobeyed; condition broken. Pay S. immediately balance of my money; allow no further expense; recall money advanced if not spent.[5]

Merriam realized the attack was imminent. With the ammunition, Brown had the final resources he needed. But John Anderson, Hayden's other recruit, had not arrived. In Merriam's mind Anderson had disobeyed orders, possibly deserted. In reality, Anderson may have gotten lost, or he may have fallen into the hands of slave hunters. Merriam's instructions to Hayden were direct: It's too late to send more recruits. Don't waste the money. Give whatever money is left, and whatever you can recover, to "S"—Sanborn.

This may not have been the only telegram from Merriam to Hayden. A few days after Brown's attack, Wendell Phillips wrote to Sanborn regarding "Our friend who received telegrams. . . ."[6] Sanborn could only conclude that "Our friend" was Hayden. Later on, at the time of his death, a New York newspaper described Hayden's home, where "in the front parlor under the carpet were secreted the telegrams sent from time to time giving an account of the progress of [Brown's] raid."[7]

Merriam was the final volunteer to join Brown's army. Brown

now had twenty-one soldiers, sixteen whites and five blacks. Captain Brown was ready to attack.

On Sunday evening, October 16, 1859, John Brown gave his men their final orders. Merriam and two other recruits were to stay behind, to guard the rifles, pistols, and pikes stockpiled for the free blacks and the slaves Brown hoped would join his rebellion. Brown discussed the attack and warned his men not to spill blood needlessly but to defend themselves as necessary. Then he faced his small army and gave the command, "Men, get on your arms; we will proceed to the Ferry."[8] Their target was the federal arsenal at Harper's Ferry, Virginia.

Initially the attack went well. Brown and his men were in control of the arsenal by dawn on Monday. The band waited for relief from the uprising their commander was sure would develop. The armed men streaming into Harper's Ferry on Monday morning, however, were not slaves and free blacks but local farmers determined to kill the rebels holding the arsenal. By noon, Brown and his men were hopelessly surrounded. Shots rang out throughout the day.

By Tuesday morning, the arsenal was encircled by a detachment of United States Marines who had arrived during the night. Eight of Brown's raiders and three local citizens were already dead or dying. When Brown refused to surrender, Lieutenant J. E. B. Stuart led the final assault, killing two more raiders and capturing Brown and six of his men.

Merriam and those left behind with the extra weapons were able to escape. Merriam returned to Concord but panic had already set in among Brown's former supporters. Sanborn refused to see the man he had sent to Brown, but asked his sister to help. She turned Merriam over to Henry Thoreau. Using an assumed name, Thoreau took the fugitive to the train station and gave him a ticket to Canada.

After imprisoning Brown and the surviving raiders, authorities searched Brown's rented farm. In addition to the stockpile of weapons, they found Brown's notes and maps, together with letters from Franklin Sanborn, Gerrit Smith, Samuel Howe, and the copy of Lewis Hayden's letter that John Brown, Jr. had sent to his father.

The New York Herald published all these letters on October 25. Most of Brown's friends, reading their "secret" letters in the newspapers, were terrified, afraid of being arrested and standing trial with Brown. Across New England that fall, Brown's friends stoked their parlor fires with letters they had received from the captain and from each other.

But destruction of evidence was not enough. Smith became so hysterical his friends had him declared insane and confined in the state asylum. Sanborn, Howe, and Stearns left for Canada. Douglass fled to Europe. Theodore Parker was already in Europe, where he had been traveling since June.

Only Hayden and Higginson waited for the consequences. Higginson hoped he would be arrested, or at least called to testify, but the summons never came. Hayden was not called to testify at Brown's trial, but when a select committee of the United States Senate met in January of 1860 to investigate "the late invasion and seizure of public property at Harper's Ferry," it issued a summons for Lewis Hayden to testify.

The summons was never served. After issuing the summons, James M. Mason, senator from Virginia and committee chairman, learned that Hayden was black and for that reason Mason instructed the United States Marshal to withhold the summons.

Brown and six of his raiders were tried for murder and for treason against the state of Virginia. They were found guilty and sentenced to death.

John Brown was executed by hanging on December 2, 1859. On the day of his execution, Brown left behind a last note:

> I, John Brown, am now quite certain that the crimes of this guilty land will never be purged away; but with blood. I had, as I now think vainly, flattered myself that without very much bloodshed; it might be done.[9]

Four of Brown's men followed him to the gallows on December 16. Two more were executed on March 16, 1860. Of the twenty-two men in John Brown's army, ten died in the attempt to capture the arsenal. Seven were executed. Only five escaped.

John Brown's raid was a tactical failure, but his deed widened the gulf between North and South. His statements before the court, the letters he wrote from prison, and his courage before death made him a martyr for those opposed to slavery. His sacrifice called on every reformer to increase his or her commitment to the anti-slavery cause. Speaking in Brooklyn, New York, Wendell Phillips explained Brown's role:

> There is no cowardice in Virginia. The South are not cowards. . . . Virginia did not tremble at an old gray-headed man at Harper's Ferry; they trembled at a John Brown in every man's own conscience.[10]

Even William Lloyd Garrison offered praise. The great editor's opinions were not converted by Brown's attack, but he could express sympathy for Brown's purpose. "I am a non-resistant," Garrison declared in a speech in Boston, on the day of Brown's execution, "yet as a peace man—an ultra peace man—I am prepared to say, 'Success to every slave insurrection at the South, and in every slave country.' "[11]

Southerners were terrified, sure Brown's raid was only the first of many attacks organized by Northern abolitionists. Southerners read of Garrison's statement that between Virginia and himself there was an "irrepressible conflict" and he, the non-resistant, was for "carrying it on until it is finished in victory or death."[12] A committee of the Virginia legislature, investigating John Brown's attack, reported that a conspiracy existed, "not merely against Virginia, but against the peace and security of all Southern states."[13]

Many Southerners believed that, while it was one thing for abolitionists to attack federal marshals in Boston, it was a different situation when abolitionists attacked a peaceful community and murdered unarmed citizens as they did at Harper's Ferry. Perhaps it was time for those who supported slavery to part company with those who opposed it.

Eleven months after Brown's death, Northern voters elected Abraham Lincoln president of the United States. Although Lincoln lost in every state that permitted slavery, and he failed to receive a majority of the national vote, his victories in the eighteen states that did not allow slavery gave him 59% of the electoral votes. Six weeks after Lincoln's election, South Carolina announced its secession from the Union. War was about to begin and, as John Brown's friends had hoped, slavery was about to come to an end.

Even though only one of the seven men he recruited for John Brown's army ever reached the captain, Lewis Hayden played a crucial role in Brown's raid. Hayden supported Brown when others had lost faith, and his recruit, Merriam, delivered the final resources that made the attack possible. Historians have labeled Brown's committee of white supporters—Sanborn, Howe, Stearns, Parker, Smith, and Higginson—the "Secret Six." With the addition of Lewis Hayden to the committee, the label should be changed to the "Secret Seven."

13. ". . . And May Include Persons of African Descent"

When civil war broke out in April 1861, one member of the Hayden family was already serving in the armed forces. Not Lewis. At fifty years of age he was too old. It was Joseph Hayden, Lewis and Harriet's son, who was enlisted in the United States Navy.

Joseph joined the Navy in November of 1857 giving his occupation as "barber" and his place of birth as "Michigan."[1] Since Joseph technically remained a fugitive slave under federal law, he avoided difficult questions by giving a free state, rather than Kentucky, as his place of birth.

The United States Navy had enlisted blacks since its earliest years, but most blacks were denied full status as "seaman" and served as cooks, stewards, cabin boys, or in other menial jobs. Joseph was initially assigned the rank of "landsman," an inexperienced sailor. When he reenlisted with two-and-a-half years of experience, he was still a landsman.

Joseph was able to see a large portion of the world courtesy of the Navy. Aboard the *Vandalia*, he traveled along the coast of South America and cruised the Pacific Ocean, visiting the Fiji Islands and Pitcairn Island. When the Civil War erupted, the

Vandalia returned to the Atlantic Ocean and joined other Union ships blockading the harbor at Charleston, South Carolina.

Joseph may have joined the Navy in 1857 due to a lack of employment opportunities. In that year the United States was hit by an economic "panic," which today we would call a depression. As overbuilt railroads failed and land speculators went bankrupt, businesses faltered and banks collapsed.

Among the casualties of the panic was Lewis Hayden's clothing store. Hayden closed his store on Cambridge Street in 1858 and moved to smaller quarters. Shortly after the move the new store burned, and Hayden was reduced to peddling jewelry. Fortunately his years of friendship with prominent men soon provided a new opportunity.

The previous year, Hayden had convinced his longtime friend John Andrew to run for the Massachusetts legislature. Andrew had a reputation as a poor man's lawyer and had represented many of Boston's blacks without a fee. Since men of African descent could vote in Boston but could not hold public office, the men of the Sixth Ward (where many of Boston's black citizens lived) wanted Andrew to represent them.

The Whig party had dominated the Ward in previous elections and Andrew allowed Hayden to submit his name for the Republican ticket. The Republican party was relatively new, many of its members were former Whigs from the North who had tired of the compromises intended to preserve slavery and the Union. As its first national issue, the Republican party had committed itself to opposing slavery in the rapidly growing western territories. Even Hayden doubted Andrew could win with the new party, but to their surprise, he was elected. Afterwards he chided Hayden, "Had I known that I would have been elected, I never would have allowed the use of my name."[2]

After Andrew's upset victory, Hayden was recognized as a significant figure in Republican politics. When hard times came in 1858, influential Republicans secured Hayden a position as a messenger in the office of the Massachusetts secretary of state. The position of "messenger" was not lofty, but the appointment was significant. Until this time government service was not open to persons of African descent and Hayden became the first black government employee in Massachusetts and a model for those who would follow. Near the seat of political power for the next thirty years, Hayden had the ear of an entire generation of governors and state legislators.

Hayden's best friend in the state legislature, John Andrew, refused to run for a second term. Yet even Andrew's withdrawal from elected office could not prevent the expansion of his political career. On November 18, 1859, Andrew presided over a meeting to raise funds for the families of the imprisoned Harper's Ferry raiders. Andrew was not a radical abolitionist, but John Brown's raid had moved him. He stirred the crowd by declaring he would not consider, "whether the enterprise of John Brown and his associates in Virginia was wise or foolish, right or wrong; I only know that whether the enterprise was one or the other, *John Brown himself is right.*"[3]

With encouragement from his friends, Andrew reentered politics in 1860 as a delegate to the Republican national convention in Chicago that nominated Abraham Lincoln for president. Later that summer, Massachusetts Republicans were surprised when the incumbent governor declined their renomination. The party quickly nominated Andrew for governor, and he easily won the office on the same ticket that elected Lincoln as president.

When war broke out between the Union and the states of the Confederacy in 1861, Massachusetts, under Andrew's leadership,

John A. Andrew was Republican war-governor of Massachusetts and Hayden's friend. He followed Hayden's promptings to form a regiment of black soldiers as soon as the Emancipation Proclamation went into effect.

was among the first and the most generous in the sending of forces. As troops marched through the streets of Boston on their way to southern battlefields, Hayden and other black leaders were disturbed. In a war fought between states that opposed slavery and those that supported it, Union leaders denied the former slaves and their friends the right to take up arms.

In April, only two weeks after the Confederate attack on Fort Sumter, Hayden and Robert Morris addressed a meeting of Boston's black citizens. Denied the "privilege of forming a part of the militia," the participants were determined to show that they were ready to fight. Inspired by the speeches, 125 black men joined a drill company to prepare for military service.[4]

Abolitionist leaders, black and white, pressed federal and state officials to allow black men into the army. In May, sympathetic Massachusetts legislators introduced a resolution urging the federal government to enlist men of African descent. The resolution passed in the Massachusetts Senate but was narrowly defeated in the House.

On the federal level, President Lincoln and other Union leaders were reluctant to arm former slaves. Four slave states (Delaware, Maryland, Kentucky, and Missouri) and the western counties of Virginia (now the state of West Virginia) had not seceded. Union leaders feared that arming former slaves might increase sympathy for the Confederacy in the slave states still loyal to the Union.

As the war dragged into its second year, however, Union casualties mounted and Confederate generals demonstrated they were more than a match for their Northern counterparts. In response, Lincoln's advisors called for a policy that would reenergize the Union mission and deny slave labor to the South.

In September 1862, President Lincoln announced that effective January 1, 1863, slaves would be free in those areas held by the Confederacy. The Emancipation Proclamation would not free slaves in the border states loyal to the Union, but as Union armies moved forward, slaves in newly liberated areas would be freed. The policy gave the war a new purpose and made it clear that the end of slavery in the United States was near.

If the end of slavery was near, so was the beginning of military service for the former slaves and their friends. By November 1862, Hayden's friend Wentworth Higginson was in command of the First South Carolina Volunteers, a regiment of former slaves known as "contrabands" because they had been taken from their former owners as the spoils of war. In Kansas, Richard Hinton, a John Brown follower who had not been at Harper's Ferry, organized an independent regiment of escaped slaves. Despite these efforts, no free state had offered to include blacks in its regiments.

Just six weeks before the Emancipation Proclamation was to take effect, Harriet and Lewis Hayden invited their friend, Governor

John Andrew, to their home for Thanksgiving dinner. Thanksgiving was an important holiday in Massachusetts, the Pilgrim State, and it was not a small gesture for the governor to celebrate the day with former slaves. Hayden wrote Andrew a formal note:

Boston, November 25, 1862

Please not to forget to call at Lewis Hayden's house 66 Southack Street, at 4-1/2 o'clock on the afternoon of Thursday the 27th instant.
Most respectfully yours,
Lewis Hayden[5]

The governor's visit created excitement, but the observation of a black barber revealed Hayden's standing in the community. When asked by a customer if it was true that the governor would dine at the Hayden home, the barber commented, "I reckon it's so. Lewis Hayden ain't a mite proud. He'd just as soon set down and eat with a governor as with anybody else."[6]

Hayden did not invite Governor Andrew to dinner as a social gesture. He had a purpose, and that purpose was the formation of a regiment of black soldiers. Despite the friendship between the two men, the debate at the Thanksgiving table must have been lively. Hayden knew the importance of former slaves fighting for their own freedom and he knew his friends were willing to fight. The Emancipation Proclamation would soon be effective and the time to enlist black men had come.

Andrew probably had other concerns. William Wells Brown wanted black regiments to have black officers, and Robert Morris thought black men should not enlist unless they were guaranteed black officers. Andrew was well aware, however, that because of

119

the Army's refusal to admit them, few black men had any military experience, let alone the experience necessary to be an officer. In addition, many white officers were saying that they would not serve if black officers were admitted as their equals. Finally, Andrew knew he would have to get permission from the Lincoln administration if the regiment was to become a part of the federal forces.

Hayden was willing to accept a compromise on the question of black officers. "I have no objection to white officers," he counseled, "so long as competent black men are eligible for promotion when they have earned it."[7] Before Andrew left that evening, Hayden had the governor's promise to seek federal permission to form a regiment of black soldiers as soon as the Emancipation Proclamation went into effect.

That happened on January 1, 1863 and, true to his word, Andrew traveled to Washington. On January 26, he met with Edwin Stanton, the secretary of war, and was shown a draft of an order authorizing the governor of Massachusetts to raise "such corps of infantry for the volunteer service as he may find convenient, such volunteers to be enlisted for three years, or until sooner discharged." Andrew read the order carefully, then remembering his promise to Hayden, he wrote on the bottom, "and may include persons of African descent, organized into separate corps."[8]

The Secretary then signed the order with Andrew's amendment. At the end of January, Andrew offered command of the new corps, to be known as the Fifty-fourth Massachusetts Regiment, to Colonel Robert Gould Shaw, a veteran of the Second Massachusetts Regiment. The first recruits reported to camp on February 21, but by the end of the month fewer than 250 men had enlisted. Organizers realized Massachusetts could not supply the 1,200 men of African descent required for a full regiment. Andrew turned to George Stearns, one of John Brown's supporters, for assistance.

Since Massachusetts was the only free state to sponsor a "colored regiment," Stearns suggested recruiters could go into the other free states to fill the ranks.[9] Black abolitionists volunteered their services. Frederick Douglass promoted the regiment in his speeches and in his newspaper, and one of his sons was among the first to enlist. William Wells Brown, Charles Lenox Remond, and Lewis Hayden, the former "agents" of the Anti-Slavery Society, became agents of the State of Massachusetts.

The recruiters went into other states and up into Canada. Canada was especially difficult because it was against the law for a foreign nation to enlist soldiers on Canadian soil. Hayden and the others were able to avoid the law by interesting men in the new regiment and then sending them to the United States to enlist. Stearns placed a physician in Buffalo, New York to examine the potential enlistees and send the able-bodied ones to Boston.

The recruiters had great success. So many men poured across the railroad lines, Stearns was able to negotiate special rates. By the end of April, volunteers were arriving at the rate of 100 per day. By the middle of May, the Fifty-fourth Massachusetts was at full strength and new recruits were being assigned to a sister regiment, the Fifty-fifth Massachusetts, under the command of Hayden's friend, Norwood Hallowell.

On May 18, 1863, Governor Andrew presented the Fifty-fourth with its battle flags. Viewing the remarkable regiment, the Governor declared, "I stand or fall, as a man and a magistrate, with the rise and fall in history of the Fifty-fourth Massachusetts Regiment."[10]

Ten days later the regiment paraded through the streets of Boston with 1,364 enlisted men and seventy-eight officers. All the

Shame and Gallantry

The inclusion of black soldiers in the Union army was not without disappointment. Enlisted men of African descent were segregated into "colored regiments" where almost all their officers were whites. In addition, many commanders wished to limit these new regiments to garrison duty—menial tasks such as clearing roads and gathering firewood—thus saving white soldiers for battle duty.

The most galling insult was that federal officials refused to pay the new recruits as soldiers. Enlisted soldiers at that time were paid $13 per month. After the Fifty-fourth Regiment had commenced enlistments, federal officials revealed that they intended to pay black recruits as laborers at the rate of $10 per month. To their great credit, members of the Fifty-fourth and other black regiments continued to enlist and to serve, but would not accept less than full military pay. Lewis Hayden, George Stearns, Frederick Douglass, Colonel Robert Shaw, and Governor John Andrew all labored hard and long to correct the situation.

The members of the Fifty-fourth and Fifty-fifth Regiments were so adamant about the issue of pay that when the Massachusetts legislature volunteered to make up the difference, the soldiers refused the offer, demanding that the federal government honor its obligation. The matter was finally resolved in June 1864 when full pay was given to the soldiers, retroactive to their enlistment dates.

Despite their shameful treatment by federal officials, black

After the success of Massachusetts's regiments of black soldiers, the federal government organized over 125,000 men into units of "U.S. Colored Troops." These men of the 107th Infantry Regiment stood guard at Fort Corcoran near Washington, D.C. Courtesy of the Massachusetts Commandery Military Order of the Loyal Legion and the US Army Military History Institute

soldiers served gallantly. The most shining example was an attack in July of 1863 by the Fifty-fourth Massachusetts Regiment. Less than sixty days after departing their training ground, the regiment was part of a force attempting to capture Fort Wagner, on the South Carolina coast.

On the evening of July 18, the regiment made a desperate charge along the beaches and into the Confederate guns. The Fifty-fourth planted its colors upon the rampart of the fort and it was there that the regiment's commander, Colonel Shaw, was killed. Outnumbered, with casualties mounting, and without reinforcements, the unit fell back to a forward position until relieved the next morning. At the end of the attack three officers and ninety-three enlisted men were dead or missing. One hundred fifty more men were wounded or captured.

In the final two years of the war, more than 180,000 men of African descent served in the Union forces. Only 109 of these men were commissioned as officers—a very small number—but the barrier had been broken. In addition, twenty-four black soldiers received the Medal of Honor, the nation's highest award for bravery in combat.

enlisted men were black; all the officers, except the chaplain, were white; yet the men of the Fifty-fourth Regiment proudly marched as one, displaying the colors of their nation and their state. Thousands of onlookers cheered from sidewalks, rooftops, and windows.

More than one observer remembered the day in 1854 when a troop of white soldiers and thugs marched a single black man, Anthony Burns, through the streets of Boston to return him to slavery. Nine years later fourteen hundred men, many of them former slaves, marched through the same streets offering their lives to put an end to slavery.

The Fifty-fifth Regiment was soon filled and on July 21, 1863, Massachusetts' second regiment of African American soldiers left camp for southern battlefields. Five months later, Massachusetts announced that it would form a third unit composed of men of African descent, the Fifth Regiment Massachusetts Cavalry. Hayden recruited in Pennsylvania and Ohio for that unit. Some reports indicate Hayden also recruited in Kansas and, after his death, the *Boston Transcript* stated that Hayden even "went through the Union lines on recruiting service South."[11]

Certainly Lewis Hayden was one of the first to advocate including men of African descent in the Union army, but others advocated the same idea. The concept of a regiment of black soldiers is too obvious to argue who first suggested it. Hayden's distinction is that he succeeded; he brought the Fifty-fourth Massachusetts Regiment to life in January 1863, by lobbying for the plan to the right person, his friend, Governor Andrew, at the right time—just before the effective date of the Emancipation Proclamation.

In all, approximately 350,000 Union soldiers died in the war that brought freedom to four million slaves. Among the Union dead were 36,000 black soldiers. On the Confederate side, approximately 250,000 men died trying to defend the status quo. As John Brown had predicted, the crime of slavery was finally purged away with bloodshed, "very much bloodshed."

The end of the war did not mark the end of slavery in every state. Since slaves in the border states had not been liberated by the Emancipation Proclamation, they continued to suffer after many of their brothers and sisters in the Confederate states had been freed by the Union army. Maryland and Missouri, slave states that had remained with the Union, abolished slavery before the end of the war. And, although the institution of slavery had virtually collapsed by the end of the war, it was not outlawed in Hayden's home state of Kentucky until ratification of the Thirteenth Amendment to the Constitution in December 1865.

The abolitionists' immediate goal, the end of slavery in the United States, had been accomplished. The battle for equality was just beginning, but for a short time at least, they could rejoice in their victory, however bloody.

The Hayden family had little time for rejoicing. In the summer of 1865, Lewis and Harriet received word that their son, Joseph, was dead at the age of twenty-eight years.

When Joseph's initial enlistment expired in November 1861, he reenlisted for a three-year term, still giving his place of birth as Michigan. He was assigned to the USS *Stockdale* and then to the USS *Fort Gaines*. Both vessels were steam patrol boats operating in Admiral David Farragut's fleet in the Mississippi River delta and along the Gulf coast. Naval records indicate that Joseph was discharged at the end of his three-year term, on December 10, 1864.

Joseph Hayden died at Fort Morgan, Alabama, on June 27, 1865.

How or why he died is unknown. He may have died from lingering military wounds. He may have died from violence not related to the war. Most likely he died of one of the many diseases that killed more men in the Civil War than bullets, bayonets, and cannon balls combined.

14. "A Prince Among Us"

The end of the Civil War brought the end of slavery in the United States, and Lewis Hayden turned his attention to the fight for equality. In the years after the war, Hayden spent a great deal of his time promoting and defending black participation in the Freemason movement. He realized that through fraternal organizations, like the Freemasons, blacks could help one another in business and socially. In 1866, Hayden wrote an important essay, "Caste among Masons," that attacked racism in the Freemason movement. As grand master (president) of his Masonic lodge, he visited Virginia and South Carolina in order to establish lodges for blacks in those states.

After the Civil War, blacks were allowed to hold public office in Massachusetts and, in 1873, friends urged Hayden to run for the Massachusetts legislature. He was easily elected from the ward that had elected John Andrew fifteen years earlier. Like Andrew, Hayden was a reluctant politician and served only one term. Although he was not the first black elected to the Massachusetts legislature, Hayden was one of the first.

Whether serving in the legislature, working in the state house, or meeting with his neighbors, Hayden was a forceful leader in the

Lewis Hayden, in about 1873, as a Massachusetts state legislator.
By permission of the Massachusetts Historical Society, Boston

black community and was well respected by the political leaders of Massachusetts. One author reported that during the postwar years, "Hayden was a man of compelling qualities and of a nature that would not brook opposition. With the Negroes he held a position almost of dictator, and with the Whites he was the accepted representative of his people." These words were published in 1914, when some of the men and women who had known Hayden were still alive to have their opinions recorded.[1]

Despite his popularity with political leaders, Hayden did not hesitate to take on anyone who disagreed with his philosophy. In March 1888, the *New York Age* published an engraving of Hayden and described him as "Father Hayden, the old philosopher of the State House." Accompanying the engraving was a lengthy article praising Hayden as a man whose efforts had "won for him widespread respect among all classes of citizens," but the writer had to admit that Hayden was "never mealy mouthed" and was

> an ultra stalwart Republican who believed that a Northern Democrat . . . whether he was a white or black man, was responsible for the outrages committed upon the colored people of the South, equally with the most pronounced rebels.[2]

Hayden saw a link between the forces that oppressed blacks and the forces that oppressed women. Although his friends often remembered him as an advocate of women's rights, few concrete examples of his efforts can be cited other than a letter he wrote to James Freeman Clarke, a Unitarian minister. In the 1840s and 1850s Clarke had been a friend of Henry David Thoreau, Ralph Waldo Emerson, and other enlightened thinkers. When Boston ministers shunned Theodore Parker because of his radical ideas,

Clarke invited Parker to preach in his church. In 1887, Hayden wrote to Clarke and his wife, reminiscing about their struggles:

> How well I remember Mr. Clarke's writing and advocacy of the rights of my race to freedom and equal manhood, as well as his devotion to the cause of woman; for he and I know that as long as man lauds it over her our country is not free; day by day however the strength of her oppressors is being weakened, and like slavery this wrong must give way too, for right shall triumph.[3]

The passing years brought down the curtain on the era of the abolitionists as death claimed them. In May 1879, Hayden was a pallbearer at the funeral of William Lloyd Garrison, and in February 1884 Hayden served as pallbearer at Wendell Phillips's funeral. When William Wells Brown died in November 1884, Hayden was asked to give one of the funeral addresses. Like Hayden, Brown had been born a slave in Lexington, Kentucky, and like Hayden, Brown had escaped from slavery through Ohio's Underground Railroad.

Brown had been a forceful speaker and an accomplished writer on behalf of the anti-slavery movement. In his writings, Brown described Hayden as "one of the most faithful friends of his race, daring everything for freedom, never shrinking from any duty, and never counting the cost." Brown had also pointed out that while he "does not attempt to be an orator, Mr. Hayden is, nevertheless, a very effective speaker."[4] No doubt Hayden used his abilities as "a very effective speaker" to return the compliments at Brown's funeral.

In 1887, despite the recognition and the honors coming to him, despite his thirty years of service in the state house, and despite being over seventy years old, Hayden still had one more battle to fight. He was determined to see Massachusetts recognize a former slave of mixed race as a hero of the American Revolution. The former slave was Crispus Attucks, one of five men killed in the Boston Massacre of 1770.

———————

Tempers were short that long-ago winter in Boston. British soldiers were quartered in the city to enforce the hated customs regulations. Each day brought new reports of verbal and physical confrontations between colonists and soldiers. On the night of March 5, 1770, a crowd of Bostonians cornered a British officer and eight enlisted men against a wall of the Customs House.

Almost fifty years old and standing six feet, two inches, Crispus Attucks was the leader of a group of sailors that joined the crowd in taunting the British "lobster backs." As the crowd launched missiles of sticks, ice, and snow, the soldiers leveled their muskets. Members of the crowd shouted at the soldiers and cursed them, daring them to fire.

"Damn you, you rascals, fire!" someone called from the crowd. "You dare not fire!" called another.[5]

A large stick flew through the air and knocked a British private to the ground. Rising to his feet, he fired his musket. The other enlisted men followed suit. By the time the British officer had regained control, Attucks and three other men were dead. A fifth man was dying. Six men were wounded.

Three days later, Bostonians held an enormous funeral for the victims of the "Boston Massacre." Every shop in Boston was closed for mourning. Ten thousand people marched with the bodies of the martyrs to the Old Granary Burying Ground.

Samuel Adams used the event to demand the removal of the British troops from Boston. Given the size of the crowds and the temper of the city, British officials agreed and moved their regiments to Castle William, an island fortress in Boston Harbor, where the British regiments remained until 1774.

After the Revolution, Bostonians honored the Boston Massacre as the first blood spilled in the struggle for American independence. Black Bostonians honored Attucks's martyrdom as proof of their contribution to the American nation.

In 1851 seven black leaders, including Lewis Hayden and William Nell, petitioned the Massachusetts legislature for $1,500 to erect a monument to Attucks. The petition failed, but the group did not give up.

Beginning on March 5, 1858, the abolitionists sponsored annual commemorations of Attucks's death. At that first celebration in Faneuil Hall, Wendell Phillips was the featured speaker giving "honor to one of the first martyrs in our Revolution." The Boston Massacre did not come *before* the Revolution, he asserted: it was the beginning of the Revolution" "Who taught the British soldier that he might be defeated? Who dared first to look into his eyes? Those five men! The fifth of March was the baptism of blood. The fifth of March was what made the Revolution something besides talk . . . I hail the fifth of March as the baptism of the Revolution into forcible resistance; without that it would have been simply a discussion of rights."

Then, to the delight of his audience, Phillips predicted a memorial would be raised to Attucks. "The time will yet come when we will . . . drag this Massachusetts Legislature at our heels, and they shall pay for a monument to Attucks. It will be the magnanimous atonement for the injury and forgetfulness of so many years. You and I, faithful to our trust, will see to it."[6]

Phillips did not live to see a monument to Attucks, but in his determined manner, Hayden resolved that *he* would. In over thirty years of trying, Boston's black community was unable to get an Attucks monument. As practical as he was strong-willed, Hayden proposed the workable solution. If Massachusetts would not erect a monument to the one man of African descent among the five massacred colonists, Massachusetts could not resist a request to erect a monument to all five martyrs.

In the spring of 1887, Hayden and other community leaders, both black and white, presented a petition to the Massachusetts legislature requesting a monument erected in memory of "Crispus Attucks, Samuel Gray, Jonas Caldwell, and Samuel Maverick, who, together with Patrick Carr, led by Crispus Attucks, were the first martyrs in the cause of American Liberty, having been shot by the British soldiers on the night of fifth of March, A.D. 1770, known as the Boston Massacre." Many notable names were on the petition, including Dr. Henry Bowditch and Hugh O'Brien, mayor of Boston, but the first name on the petition was Lewis Hayden.[7]

The legislature approved funds for a monument to the five martyrs to be placed on Boston Common, a large park in the heart of Boston. Hayden served on the dedication committee, and when it took place on November 14, 1888, he was among the dignitaries seated on the platform.

Observers that day could not help but compare Crispus Attucks, who had defied British soldiers, with Lewis Hayden, who had defied the United States government and the Fugitive Slave Law. George W. Putnam, an artist and a friend of many prominent abolitionists, saw a great difference, however, between the two. Putnam recalled his conversations with men who had visited the Hayden home in 1850 when Hayden, his son, Joseph, and William Craft were barricaded inside to protect Craft from the United States marshals.

I thought that Lewis Hayden was a much greater man than Crispus Attucks for I have little doubt that if Crispus had had the least idea of getting killed on that occasion [the day of the massacre] he would have made tracks to a place of safety, but brave Lewis Hayden faced a nation of foes and all the military power of that Nation, never for a moment expecting to outlive the attacks but determined and willing to die for human freedom![8]

Hayden was proud of the monument and his role in obtaining it. After the dedication he told his friends, "I am happy and ready to die now. They cannot take from us this record of history showing that we participated in the revolution to secure American liberty, as we have participated in every great movement in the best interests of the country since."[9]

In creating the monument to the victims of the Boston Massacre, in recruiting the final dollars for John Brown's raid, and in lobbying John Andrew for the creation of regiments of black soldiers—Hayden succeeded where others had failed. In each of these events, the former slave, dismissed by the American Anti-Slavery Society as an ineffective public speaker, provided the wisdom and the energy to transform a vision into a reality.

The dedication of the Boston Massacre monument, which still stands in Boston Common, was the last official act of Hayden's life. Almost eighty years old, he suffered from kidney disease and sat with great difficulty on the public platform that day. After the dedication, he still worked in the secretary of state's office as much as his health permitted, and he moved through the statehouse known and respected by everyone he met.

As Hayden's health continued to fail he never complained about his suffering, but his friends noticed he seemed bothered by external problems. Early in 1889, Dr. Henry Bowditch, Lewis's friend for forty years, questioned Harriet Hayden.

"Lewis seems somewhat distressed. Is he comfortable about his money affairs?"

"Ah, doctor! Were he relieved of those he would be at comparative peace."

Bowditch found out that his friend worried about the mortgage on his home.

"It is a shame that a man who has been so excellent in every relation of life should be distressed about money in his last hours," responded Bowditch.[10]

Bowditch gathered a committee to assist the Haydens. Among the first to volunteer was Norwood Hallowell, former commander of the Fifty-fifth Massachusetts Regiment. Friends gave generously to a fund, and the committee paid the mortgage on the historic home at 66 Phillips Street as well as the Haydens' other debts. (The street name had been changed from Southac to Phillips.) In addition, Bowditch presented Harriet with $1,500 to invest for the future.

Financial security was a great relief to Hayden. As a token of his gratitude, Hayden offered Bowditch the gold watch he had used to regulate his appointments in the statehouse. At first Bowditch refused, but Harriet insisted and Bowditch accepted the gift. Later Bowditch considered selling the watch and adding the amount to Harriet's investments but she would not consent. Bowditch gratefully resolved to wear his friend's watch for the rest of his life.

Lewis Hayden died at home on Sunday morning, April 7, 1889. In reporting Hayden's death, the Boston newspapers competed for the most complete versions of his life and commentaries from the most important persons. Hayden's death was front page news for the *Boston Herald*, the *Boston Globe*, the *Boston Evening Transcript*, the *New York Times*, and many other newspapers.

Hayden's funeral was held on Thursday, April 11. The *Boston Globe* reported the funeral was, "the greatest tribute of love, honor, and respect ever shown any colored man in the United States." That morning, hundreds of friends and members of fraternal organizations gathered to escort Hayden's casket from his home to the church. Twelve hundred mourners gathered in the church and hundreds more stood outside.

The funeral was one last gathering for the remaining abolitionists. Thomas Wentworth Higginson, Franklin Sanborn, and Henry Bowditch were there. Norwood Hallowell and Francis Jackson Garrison, son of William Lloyd Garrison, were among the pallbearers. Lucy Stone and Frederick Douglass were there. The governor of Massachusetts, the secretary of state, the mayor of Boston, the chief of police, and the police commissioner all attended. Delivering the formal eulogy, the Reverend J. P. Jenifer enumerated Hayden's efforts against slavery, and against segregated schools, for temperance, for women's suffrage, and for the black Masons. Finally, the minister summarized Hayden's life:

> The secret of the success in Lewis Hayden's life is that he lived for others. He was, indeed, a prince among us. He has done his work well; he has passed over the river, and he has joined that band of heroes who stood up for the race when it was unable to stand for itself. They are nearly all gone; a few are left; soon they too will be gone.

Special guests were then called on to add their observations. Lucy Stone, the advocate for women's rights, spoke, but unfortunately her remarks were not recorded. Former mayor Hugh O'Brien told the mourners, "It was a benediction in the Mayor's office to have a visit from Lewis Hayden."

Higginson spoke at length, taking great care to give his friend proper credit in the rescue of Shadrach and the attempts to rescue Sims and Burns. But for Higginson himself, Hayden's actions had a special meaning:

> Lewis Hayden taught a lesson to a whole nation, that the nation needed, that the abolitionists, and especially the colored abolitionists, were not cowards. Most of those who are before me cannot go back to the time when the streets of Boston were far different from what they are now.
>
> All the colored soldiers love to recall the day when Lewis Hayden sat in that room with revolvers and dirks, waiting for the slaveholder to break into the house. It is in recognition of that service that we . . . are glad to be here and to cast our leaf in his memory.[11]

William Lloyd Garrison II added his tribute, saying, "this slave by birth was an honor to freedom," and pointing out that, "the press that 30 years ago would have chronicled with satisfaction 'one Negro less,' [now] displays his portrait and tells his virtues in ample and respectful phrase." On behalf of his deceased father, Garrison thanked Hayden for support "when friends were few and need was great."[12] Henry Bowditch, deeply moved by the loss of his friend, spoke briefly, and, he felt, "unsatisfactorily." That evening the great physician, by then recognized as a national pioneer in the area of public health, wrote in his journal, "I never felt so oppressed before an audience, and I feel it now; as if I had lost in his death a great hold on life . . . Without the idea I shall meet him again, I feel intensely saddened."[13]

Hayden's testimonials were not limited to the funeral. Frederick Douglass and Lewis Hayden were never close, yet Douglass felt it necessary to interrupt a speech in Washington, D.C. on April 16, 1889, to mourn Hayden's passing:

> Our cause, like so many other good causes, has its ebbs and flows, successes and failures, joyous hopes and saddening fears. I cannot forget on this occasion that Lewis Hayden, a brave and wise counselor in the cause of our people, a moral hero, has laid down his armor, filled up the measure of his days, completed his work on earth, and left a mournful void in our ranks.[14]

EPILOGUE

Harriet Hayden lived for four years after Lewis's death. One of her few public appearances came upon the death of Henry Bowditch in January 1892. Prior to the funeral, the coffin was placed in the library of his home. Bowditch's son, Vincent, affectionately recorded Harriet's visit:

> The widow of his old friend, Lewis Hayden, came to the house, although old, and a cripple from rheumatism. She ascended the stairs with difficulty, and asked to be allowed to look at my father's face. As she stood by the coffin she said, with deep feeling, but as if to herself, "You dear old saint! If it had not been for you I should have been in the streets. . . ." She seemed inclined to linger, and finally, a dear family friend, fearing the effect of the cold room upon her, suggested that she should come into another part of the house and rest. Turning her head a little, she said, very gently, "Don't think me queer; you know the disciples stayed and watched; let me stay here alone;" and her wish was granted.[1]

Harriet Hayden died December 24, 1893. She had appointed Norwood Hallowell as executor of her estate. Hallowell wrote a tribute to her and her husband that appeared in the *Boston Weekly Transcript* on December 29, 1893:

> The death of Harriet Hayden, widow of the late Lewis Hayden, breaks another link in the chain which now so lightly binds the happy present to the mournful past.
>
> The Haydens, father, wife and child were born slaves in Kentucky. Our thoughts involuntarily go back to that eventful evening some sixty years ago, when the young slave mother handed her baby boy into the arms of the father, and then quickly joining him began her flight to Canada. . . .
>
> And now the crowning act of Harriet Hayden's life remains to be told. Her son, an only child, died long ago in the service of the United States under Farragut. She has bequeathed her estate, valued at some four or five thousand dollars to Harvard College, to found a scholarship for the benefit of poor and deserving colored students. By the terms of the will a medical student is to be preferred. Harvard College endowed by an old slave woman from Kentucky, is food for reflection.

Harriet Bell Hayden was buried next to Lewis along the Blooming Path in the Woodlawn Cemetery in Everett, a Boston suburb.

Prologue: A Mother and Child

1. By Lewis Hayden, 1853. Printed in Harriet Beecher Stowe, *A Key to "Uncle Tom's Cabin," Presenting the Original Facts and Documents Upon Which the Story is Founded* (Boston: John P. Jewett and Co., 1853), 154–55. Reprinted in John W. Blassingame, ed. *Slave Testimony, Two Centuries of Letters, Speeches, Interviews and Autobiographies* (Baton Rouge: Louisiana State University Press, 1977; 1992), 695–97.

1. A Slave in Lexington

1. Stowe, 154–55. Blassingame, 696.

2. "Death of Lewis Hayden," *New York Age,* April 13, 1889.

3. Stanley J. Robboy and Anita W. Robboy, "Lewis Hayden: From Fugitive Slave to Statesman," *The New England Quarterly,* 46, no. 4 (December, 1973): 594.

4. Stowe, 154–55. Blassingame, 697.

5. Hayden to Sydney Howard Gay, undated, Columbia University Libraries Special Collections. See also Randolph Paul Runyon, *Delia Webster and the Underground Railroad* (Lexington: University Press of Kentucky, 1996), 114–15.

6. Stowe, 155. Blassingame, 697.

7. Robboy and Robboy, 594; "Lewis Hayden Dead," *Boston Globe,* April 7, 1889.

8. J. Winston Coleman, Jr. *Slavery Times in Kentucky* (Chapel Hill: University of North Carolina Press, 1940.) Reprint (New York: Johnson Reprint Corporation, 1970), 125–26.

2. Crossing Over Jordan

1. Calvin Fairbank, *Calvin Fairbank During Slavery Times: How He "Fought The Good Fight" to Prepare "The Way."* Edited from his manuscript. (Chicago: Patriotic Publishing Co., 1890), 46.

2. Delia A. Webster, *Kentucky Jurisprudence: A History of the Trial of Miss Delia A. Webster* (Vergennes, Vt.: E.W. Blaisdell, 1845), 51.

3. Fairbank, 46–48.

4. Webster, 52.

5. Fairbank, 7.

6. Webster, 66–67.

3. Headed for the North Star

1. Fairbank, 48.

2. Hayden to Lewis Baxter, October 27, 1844. J. Winston Coleman Jr. Kentuckiana Collection, Transylvania University Library, Lexington.

3. Daniel G. Hill, *The Freedom Seekers: Blacks in Early Canada* (Agincourt: The Book Society of Canada, 1981), 131. See also Isaac Rice, "The Bondsmen in Canada," *Liberator,* November 23, 1849.

4. Hayden to Maria Weston Chapman, May 14, 1846. In George E. Carter and C. Peter Ripley, eds., *Black Abolitionist Papers,* 1830–1865 (Sanford, N.C.: Microfilming Corporation of America, 1981), 05:0220. The original is in the Boston Public Library.

5. Hayden to Lewis Baxter, October 27, 1844.

4. His Own Master

1. Wendell Phillips, *Speeches, Lectures, and Letters, Second Series* (Boston: Lee and Shepard, 1892), 5.

2. Hayden to Sydney Howard Gay, January 21, 1846. Columbia University Libraries Special Collections. See also Runyon, 91–92.

3. *Liberator,* April 3, 1846.

4. *Liberator,* March 27, 1846.

5. *Emancipator,* May 12, 1847.

6. William Lloyd Garrison to Sydney Howard Gay, March 31, 1846. In *The Letters of William Lloyd Garrison,* ed. by Walter M. Merrill (Cambridge: Belknap Press of Harvard University Press, 1973), 3: 334–35.

7. Hayden to Maria Weston Chapman, May 14, 1846. In Carter and Ripley, 05:0220.

8. Edmund Quincy to Maria Weston Chapman, July 11, 1846. Boston Public Library.

5. On the Road for Freedom

1. *National Anti-Slavery Standard,* July 22, 1847.

2. William McFeely, *Frederick Douglass* (New York: Simon and Schuster, 1991), 100.

3. J. C. Hathaway to E. D. Hudson, June 9, 1847. University Library, University of Massachusetts at Amherst.

4. *National Anti-Slavery Standard,* November 18, 1847.

5. J. C. Hathaway to E. D. Hudson, December 28, 1847. University Library, University of Massachusetts at Amherst.

6. *National Anti-Slavery Standard,* February 3, 1848.

7. Hayden to Wendell Phillips, February, 21, 1848 in Irving H. Bartlett, *Wendell and Ann Phillips—The Community of Reform 1840–1880* (New York: W. W.

Norton, 1979), 99. Includes a copy of the original letter which is in the Houghton Library, Harvard University (bMS Am 1953 (673).

6. A New Mission

1. *Liberator,* July 13, 1849.

2. *Liberator,* September 13, 1849.

3. *Liberator,* October 4, 1850.

4. *Liberator,* October 11, 1850.

5. *Liberator,* October 18, 1850.

8. In the Fiery Furnace

1. *Liberator,* February 21, 1851. Hayden's version of the Shadrach rescue is quoted in "Lewis Hayden Dead," *Boston Daily Globe,* April 8, 1889.

2. *Liberator,* February 21, 1851.

3. *Liberator,* February 21, 1851.

4. *Liberator,* February 21, 1851.

5. *Congressional Globe,* 31st Congress, 2 Session 596–97. Quoted in Melba Porter Hay, ed. *The Papers of Henry Clay* (Lexington: University Press of Kentucky, 1991), 10:863.

6. Charles F. Adams, *Richard Henry Dana* (Boston: Houghton, Mifflin, 1891), 2:217.

7. Thomas Wentworth Higginson, "Cheerful Yesterdays V. The Slave Period," *Atlantic Monthly* 79 (1897):346. Also in T. W. Higginson, *Cheerful Yesterdays,* (Boston: Houghton, Mifflin, 1898), 140.

8. Roy E. Finkenbine, "Boston's Black Churches" in *Courage and Conscience, Black and White Abolitionists in Boston,* (Bloomington: Indiana University Press, 1993), 182.

9. Vincent Y. Bowditch, *Life and Correspondence of Henry Ingersoll Bowditch By His Son.* 1902 Reprint (Freeport, N.Y.: Books for Libraries Press, 1970), 1:221.

9. "The Temple of Refuge"

1. Edward Everett Hale, ed. *James Freeman Clarke, Autobiography, Diary and Correspondence* (Boston: Houghton, Mifflin, 1891), 193–94.

2. Bowditch, 2:350.

3. "Lewis Hayden Dead," *Boston Daily Globe,* April 8, 1889. Also Archibald H. Grimké, "Anti-Slavery Boston," *New England Magazine,* 3 (December, 1890):458.

10. "Rescue Him!"

1. Higginson, "Cheerful Yesterdays," 349. Also in Higginson, *Cheerful Yesterdays,* 147–48.

2. Higginson, "Cheerful Yesterdays," 349; and *Cheerful Yesterdays,* 149.

3. Higginson, "Cheerful Yesterdays," 350; and *Cheerful Yesterdays,* 151.

4. Higginson, "Cheerful Yesterdays," 350–51; and *Cheerful Yesterdays,* 152–53.

5. Higginson, "Cheerful Yesterdays," 351; and *Cheerful Yesterdays,* 153.

6. Higginson, *Cheerful Yesterdays,* 155.

7. Higginson, "Cheerful Yesterdays," 352; and *Cheerful Yesterdays,* 157. See also Charles Emory Stevens, *Anthony Burns, A History.* 1856. Reprint (Williamstown, Mass.: Corner House Publishers, 1973), 44.

8. The *Atlas,* as quoted in the *Liberator,* June 2, 1854.

9. *Liberator,* June 9, 1854.

10. *Boston Journal,* May 27, 1854.

11. *Boston Daily Globe,* April 8, 1889.

12. Higginson, "Cheerful Yesterdays," 353; and *Cheerful Yesterdays,* 160.

13. *Liberator,* July 21, 1854. This address, known as "Slavery in Massachusetts," is found in most editions of Thoreau's work.

11. "Men of Action"

1. Brown to Sanborn, February 24, 1858. F. B. Sanborn, *Recollections of Seventy Years* (Boston: The Gorham Press, 1909), 1:150.

2. Sanborn. Personal Reminiscences of John Brown, April 7, 1897. Sanborn Folder, Houghton Library of Harvard University. Quoted in Stephen B. Oates, *To Purge This Land With Blood* (New York: Harper & Row, 1970), 240.

3. *New York Herald,* October 25, 1859.

4. *New York Herald,* October 25, 1859.

5. F. B. Sanborn, "The Virginia Campaign of John Brown," *Atlantic Monthly,* 36 (December, 1875): 708.

12. John Brown's Army

1. Richard J. Hinton, *John Brown and his Men.* 1894. Reprint (New York: Arno Press and the New York Times, 1968), 569.

2. Sanborn, "The Virginia Campaign . . . ," 708.

3. Sanborn, "The Virginia Campaign . . . ," 707.

4. F. B. Sanborn to T. W. Higginson, October 6, 1859, Boston Public Library.

5. Sanborn, "The Virginia Campaign . . . ," 708; Hinton, 572.

6. Sanborn, *Recollections . . .* 1:191.

7. *The New York Age,* April 13, 1889.

8. Oates, 289.

9. F. B. Sanborn, *Life and Letters of John Brown.* 1885. Reprint (New York: Negro Universities Press, 1969), 620.

10. November 1, 1859. Reported in Thomas Drew, ed. *The John Brown Invasion.* 1860. Reprint (Freeport, N.Y.: Books for Library Press, 1972), 91.

11. Walter M. Merrill, *Against Wind and Tide* (Cambridge: Harvard University Press, 1963), 273.

12. Merrill, 272.

13. Oates, 322.

13. ". . . And May Include Persons of African Descent"

1. "Enlistments At Portsmouth, N.H. in 1861; Return of the United States Naval Rendezvous at Portsmouth for the Week ending Saturday, November 30th" National Archives. Gives "Previous Naval Service".

2. "Death of Lewis Hayden," *Boston Herald,* April 8, 1889.

3. Drew, 97.

4. *Liberator,* May 3, 1861.

5. Hayden to John Andrew, November 25, 1862. Massachusetts Historical Society.

6. Letter to the Editor, *Boston Evening Transcript,* April 11, 1889.

7. Frank Preston Stearns, *The Life and Public Services of George Luther Stearns.* 1907. Reprint (Philadelphia: Lippincott, 1969), 264. Frank was the son of G. L. Stearns.

8. Albert Gallatin Browne, *Sketch of the Official Life of John A. Andrew* (New York: Hurd and Houghton, 1868), 103–04.

9. Luis F. Emilio, *A Brave Black Regiment.* 1894. Reprint (New York: Bantam Books, 1992), 12–13.

10. Henry Greenleaf Pearson, *The Life of John Andrew* (Boston: Houghton, Mifflin, 1904), 2:89.

11. *Boston Transcript,* April 8, 1889.

14. "A Prince Among Us"

1. John Daniels, *In Freedom's Birthplace, A Study of the Boston Negroes* (Boston: Houghton Mifflin, 1914), 454.

2. "Philosopher of the Hub," *New York Age,* March 31, 1888.

3. Hayden to "Rev. James Freeman Clarke & Wife," March 20, 1887, Houghton

Library, Harvard University (bM S Am 1569 (963)).

4. William Wells Brown, *The Rising Son.* 1874. Reprint (Miami, Fla.: Mnemosyne Publishing, 1969), 548.

5. A. J. Languth, *Patriots, The Men Who Started the American Revolution* (New York: Simon and Schuster, 1988), 138.

6. Phillips, 69–70, 74.

7. *A Memorial of Crispus Attucks, Samuel Maverick, James Caldwell, Samuel Gray, and Patrick Carr* (Boston: Boston City Council, 1889).

8. George W. Putnam to W. H. Siebert, December 27, 1893, in W. H. Siebert, *The Underground Railroad Scrapbook* (1910) 13, Houghton Library, Harvard University(US5278.36.25). Putnam recommended Siebert "should (at once) write to the widow of Lewis Hayden, Phillips St., Boston" for photos and additional information. Unfortunately for Siebert and other historians, Harriet had died three days earlier.

9. *New York Age,* April 13, 1889.

10. Bowditch, 2:353.

11. Unless otherwise noted the quotations from Hayden's funeral are from the *Boston Globe,* April 11, 1889.

12. Address by William Lloyd Garrison II at the funeral of Lewis Hayden, April 11. 1889. Sophia Smith Collection, Smith College, Northampton, Mass.

13. Bowditch, 2:352.

14. John W. Blassingame and John R. McKivigan, eds. *The Frederick Douglass Papers* (New Haven: Yale University Press, 1992), 5:404–05.

Epilogue

1. Bowditch, 2:369.

CHRONOLOGY
of the Life of Lewis Hayden

c.1811	Lewis Hayden born, Lexington, Kentucky.
1825	Witnesses Lafayette's visit to Lexington.
1826	Traded to Elijah Warner for a carriage and two horses.
1829	Bequeathed to Warner's daughter.
c.1839	Marries Harriet Bell.
1842	Acquired by Thomas Grant and Lewis Baxter.
1844	Calvin Fairbank and Delia Webster help the Haydens escape to Canada.
1845	Leaves Canada and resettles in Detroit with family; helps John Mifflin Brown raise money to build an African Methodist Episcopal church; travels to Boston with Brown for the first time.
1846	Addresses anti-slavery meetings with W. L. Garrison, Wendell Phillips, and other abolitionists.
1847	Becomes a traveling agent of the American Anti-Slavery Society.
1848	Fired as traveling agent; returns to Detroit.
1849	Moves to Boston with family and establishes boardinghouse; opens clothing store and raises

	$650 to ransom Calvin Fairbank.
1850	President Fillmore signs Fugitive Slave Law; Hayden defends William and Ellen Craft.
1851	Leads rescue of Shadrach; efforts to rescue Thomas Sims fail.
1853	Harriet Beecher Stowe visits Hayden boardinghouse.
1854	Anthony Burns arrested. Hayden and T. W. Higginson lead attack on courthouse but fail to rescue Burns.
1857	Joseph Hayden enlists in the Navy. Hayden helps John Andrew win election to state legislature.
1858	Loses his store but is appointed messenger in secretary of state's office. Abolitionists hold first Crispus Attucks memorial.
1859	Raises money and recruits men for John Brown. Brown's attack at Harper's Ferry fails and he is hanged in Virginia.
1860	Abraham Lincoln elected president of the United States. John Andrew elected governor of Massachusetts.
1861	War begins between the states.
1862	Lincoln announces emancipation plan; Hayden urges Governor Andrew to enlist soldiers of African descent.
1863–64	Recruits black men for Massachusetts regiments.
1865	Joseph Hayden dies at Fort Morgan, Alabama.
1873	Elected to Massachusetts legislature.
1888	Dedication of memorial to the victims of the Boston Massacre (including Crispus Attucks) in Boston Common.
1889	Lewis Hayden dies.
1893	Harriet Hayden dies.

BIBLIOGRAPHICAL ESSAY

Volumes of special interest to young adult readers are indicated as "(YA)" even if these items were prepared for general readership.

I first met Lewis Hayden in the pages of *Slavery Times in Kentucky* (YA) by J. Winston Coleman, Jr. (Chapel Hill: The University of North Carolina Press, 1940; reprint, New York: Johnson Reprint Corporation, 1970). An engineer by trade, Coleman recorded the history of black and white Kentuckians long before scholars joined the words "cultural" and "diversity." Much of the background information in chapters 1 and 2 is based on Coleman's work. Hayden's letter to Lewis Baxter in chapter 3 is a part of the J. Winston Coleman Collection at Transylvania University in Lexington.

Until this work, the only serious consideration of Hayden's life was by Stanley J. Robboy and Anita W. Robboy, "Lewis Hayden: From Fugitive Slave to Statesman," *The New England Quarterly* 46, no. 4 (December 1973): 591–613. The Robboys were infected by the Hayden legend while living in the former Hayden home at 66 Phillips Street, Boston. Their article contains a valuable compilation of sources as well as information about Hayden's Masonic career.

Hayden's description of his mother in the prologue and Rankin's trade of Hayden for a carriage and horses in chapter 1 is from *A Key to "Uncle Tom's Cabin" Presenting the Original Facts and Documents Upon Which the Story is Founded* by Harriet Beecher Stowe (Boston, 1853). That volume is rarely available, but Hayden's statement is reprinted in *Slave Testimony, Two Centuries of Letters, Speeches, Interviews, and Autobiographies* (YA) edited by John W. Blassingame (Baton Rouge: Louisiana State University Press, 1977; 1992). Elijah Warner's will is on file in the office of the Fayette County Clerk, Lexington.

Hayden's memories of Lafayette's visit to Lexington were reported in the *New York Age,* April 13, 1889. Additional information on Lafayette's visit is in *Lafayette in Kentucky* by Edgar Erskine Hume (Frankfort, Ky.: Transylvania College, 1937).

Delia Webster and Calvin Fairbank each wrote a version of the events in Lexington. Webster published an eighty-four page pamphlet shortly after leaving Kentucky, *Kentucky Jurisprudence, A History of the Trial of Miss Delia Webster* (Vergennes, Vt., 1845). Webster's version includes many court documents as well as Fairbank's letter predicting, "I shall bring out three . . .".

Fairbank published his memoirs in 1890 in *Rev. Calvin Fairbank During Slavery Times: How He "Fought the Good Fight" to "Prepare the Way"* (Chicago: Patriotic Publishing, 1890). Unfortunately, copies of Webster's pamphlet and Fairbank's book are usually available only in the special collections of major libraries. An abbreviated version of Fairbank's memoirs is in *Reminiscences of Levi Coffin.* 1898. Reprint (New York: Arno Press, 1968).

As a young history professor at Ohio State, Wilbur Henry Siebert wanted to make his courses more relevant. The professor soon realized many of his students were grandchildren of conductors on the

Underground Railroad. Siebert dedicated his life to that topic and his works include *The Underground Railroad in Massachusetts* (Worcester, Mass.: The American Antiquarian Society, 1936); *The Mysteries of Ohio's Underground Railroad* (Columbus, Ohio: Long's College Book Company, 1951); and *The Underground Railroad from Slavery to Freedom* (Gloucester, Mass.: Peter Smith, 1968). (All YA.) George Putnam's letter in chapter 14 (December 27, 1893) is from Siebert's scrapbook at the Houghton Library, Harvard University.

Research for this book was essentially complete before publication of *Delia Webster and the Underground Railroad* by Paul Runyon (Lexington: The University Press of Kentucky, 1996) but Runyon provides unique information on Hayden's first wife, Esther Harvey, and he demonstrates that Hayden's speech in "a fine grove" in Concord (chapter 4) was from the steps of Thoreau's cabin at Walden Pond.

For information on the life of former slaves in Canada see *The Freedom Seekers: Blacks in Early Canada* (YA) by Daniel G. Hill (Agincourt: The Book Society of Canada, 1981). Information about Frederick Douglass's travels with E. D. Hudson and Douglass's visit to John Brown is from *Frederick Douglass* by William McFeeley (New York: Simon and Schuster, 1991).

There are many recitals of the escape of William and Ellen Craft. William wrote his version, *Running a Thousand Miles for Freedom,* in 1860. Reprint (Miami, Fla.: Mnemosyne Publishing Co., Inc., 1969). L. Maria Child, another of the blue-blooded abolitionists, included the Crafts' story in *The Freedman's Book.* 1865. Reprint (New York: Arno Press and the New York Times, 1968).

Two versions of the Craft story are aimed at young adults: Florence B. Freedman, *Two Tickets to Freedom: The True Story of Ellen and William Craft, Fugitive Slaves,* illustrated by Ezra

Jack Keats (New York: Simon and Schuster, 1971); and Dorothy Sterling, *Black Foremothers: Three Lives* (Old Westbury, N.Y.: The Feminist Press; and New York: McGraw-Hill Book Company, 1979). For more stories of men and women escaping from slavery, see *Many Thousands Gone: African Americans from Slavery to Freedom* (YA) by Virginia Hamilton (New York: Alfred A. Knopf, 1993).

The life and rescue of Shadrach is detailed in *Shadrach Minkins, from Fugitive Slave to Citizen* by Gary Collison (Cambridge: Harvard University Press, 1997). The attempt to rescue Anthony Burns as well as additional information about his life is related in *Anthony Burns: The Defeat and Triumph of a Fugitive Slave* (YA) by Virginia Hamilton (New York: Alfred A. Knopf, 1988). Burns is treated in depth in Albert J. Von Frank, *The Trials of Anthony Burns* (Cambridge: Harvard University Press, 1998).

Direct information about the Haydens' efforts in Boston as stationmasters of the Underground Railroad is from *The Account Book of Francis Jackson, Treasurer, the Vigilance Committee of Boston* published by The Bostonian Society, n.d. *The African Meeting House in Boston, A Sourcebook* (YA) by William S. Parsons and Margaret A. Drew (Boston: The Museum of African American History, 1988) is an excellent summary of African American activity in Boston before the Civil War.

After the anti-slavery struggle, Thomas Wentworth Higginson became a respected author and frequent contributor to the *Atlantic Monthly,* which published a series of his memoirs entitled "Cheerful Yesterdays." The fifth installment ("Slave Period," *Atlantic Monthly* 79 (1897): 344–355) covers the attempts to rescue Sims and Burns. The series was gathered into a book of the same name, *Cheerful Yesterdays* by Thomas Wentworth Higginson (Boston and New York: Houghton Mifflin Company, 1898).

Higginson was the subject of a biography by Tilden G. Edelstein, *Strange Enthusiasm, A Life of Thomas Wentworth Higginson* (New Haven: Yale University Press, 1968).

For information about Theodore Parker, I used *Theodore Parker* by Henry Steele Commager (Boston: Little, Brown and Company, 1936). The description of Parker's study is from *Theodore Parker* by Octavius Brooks Frothingham (Boston: James R. Osgood and Company, 1874). In *William Lloyd Garrison and the Humanitarian Reformers* (Boston: Little, Brown and Company, 1955) Russell Nye does an excellent job of placing Garrison in historical perspective. Walter M. Merrill's biography *Against Wind and Tide* (Cambridge: Harvard University Press, 1963) is also useful.

Lewis Hayden is treated with great affection in *Life and Correspondence of Henry Ingersoll Bowditch,* by Bowditch's son, Vincent Y. Bowditch. 1902. Reprint (Freeport, N.Y.: Books for Libraries Press, 1970, two volumes). (Henry Bowditch's father, Nathaniel Bowditch, was the subject of the 1956 Newbery Medal-winning book, *Carry on Mr. Bowditch.*)

Books on John Brown could fill a small library. The best sources are from the men who knew him. Franklin B. Sanborn gathered original materials for *Life and Letters of John Brown.* 1885. Reprint (New York: Negro Universities Press, 1969). He included his own memories of Brown in *Recollections of Seventy Years* (Boston: The Gorham Press, 1909, two volumes). Sanborn also wrote an article, "The Virginia Campaign of John Brown," *Atlantic Monthly* 36 (December 1875): 704.

Richard Hinton was with Brown in Kansas but not at Harper's Ferry. Although he quotes amply from Sanborn, Hinton also presents original material in *John Brown and His Men.* 1894. Reprint (New York: Arno Press and the New York Times, 1968).

More recent works about Brown include, *To Purge This Land*

with Blood, by Stephen Oates (New York: Harper & Row, 1970); *Allies for Freedom—Blacks and John Brown,* by Benjamin Quarles (New York: Oxford University Press, 1974); *The Secret Six,* by Otto Scott (New York: Times Books, 1979); and *Ambivalent Conspirators,* by Jeffrey Rossbach (Philadelphia: University of Pennsylvania Press, 1982).

Information about black soldiers in the Massachusetts regiments is primarily from *A Brave Black Regiment* (YA) by Luis F. Emilio, an officer of the Fifty-fourth Massachusetts Regiment. 1894. Reprint (New York: Bantam Books, 1992); and *One Gallant Rush,* by Peter Burchard (New York: St. Martin's Press, 1965). The Fifty-fourth Massachusetts and the attack at Fort Wagner are also the subject of the 1989 movie *Glory.* William Gladstone offers interesting facts, lists, and photographs (but minimal narrative) in *United States Colored Troops, 1863–67* (YA) (Gettysburg, Pa.: Thomas Publications, 1990). For information about blacks in the Navy see David L. Valuska, *The African American in the Union Navy: 1861–1865* (New York: Garland Publishing, Inc., 1993). The National Archives was kind enough to provide copies of ships' muster rolls showing the naval service of Joseph Hayden.

A. J. Languth presents a dramatic retelling of the events surrounding the Boston Massacre and the death of Crispus Attucks in *Patriots, The Men Who Started the American Revolution* (New York: Simon and Schuster, 1988).

The best source of original documents on black participation in the anti-slavery movement is *The Black Abolitionist Papers* edited by C. Peter Ripley (Chapel Hill: The University of North Carolina Press, 1985–1992). This five-volume set is condensed from the more extensive Microfilm Edition of the same name (Sanford, N.C.: Microfilming Corporation of America, 1981).

The most valuable resources on the struggle to end slavery,

however, are the newspapers of the day—especially the *Liberator* and the *National Anti-Slavery Standard*. These publications are on microfilm and are available in many large libraries. A reader interested in any anti-slavery event need only check the pages of these publications two days to two weeks after the event for a full (if not unbiased) description. An afternoon spent wandering through the pages of these publications could not be regarded as wasted time.

Other newspapers provide more specific information. The *Lexington Observer and Reporter* (also on microfilm) offers ample coverage of the arrest and trial of Fairbank and Webster from the fall of 1844 through the winter of 1845. News of Hayden's death and summaries of his life fill the front pages of every Boston newspaper for the days after his death. Later that week, reports turn to coverage of Hayden's funeral including descriptions of flowers, titles of songs, and names of singers.

Many of the above items are out of print or are offered only on microfilm. Students and scholars should not hesitate to call on the interlibrary loan capabilities of their local library. An enthusiastic librarian can use the ILL system to obtain almost any published material, making the capabilities of a local library comparable to those of a large university.

ACKNOWLEDGMENTS

First and foremost, I give thanks to my wife, daughter, and son for love, patience, and encouragement. In addition to love, my brother and my mother gave helpful comments. Ed Purcell was my mentor, giving criticism and good advice in equal doses. The members of my writing group, Writers, Ink, answered revisions, rewrites, and nonsense with the barbs that are given only to those for whom one cares. Marcia Thornton Jones, Debbie Dadey, and Jerrie Oughton have given me gifts that can never be returned.

I am also indebted to James Cross Giblin, whose gift in memory of his mother, Anna, made possible the grant from The Society of Children's Book Writers and Illustrators that helped underwrite my research. My thanks to Rita and Carl Carlson for technical assistance.

In Boston, I received special assistance from Dr. Laura V. Monti and the Department of Rare Books and Manuscripts at the Boston Public Library. Philip Bergen, of the Bostonian Society, put me on Lewis Hayden's trail at an early date. Virginia H. Smith and the staff at the Massachusetts Historical Society also responded early and often. Kathi Maio of the Suffolk University Library took time to show a stranger the wonders of the sixteen-reel, microfilm edition of the *Black Abolitionist Papers*. At the Woodlawn Cemetery, Alan Giangregorio led me to Lewis's and Harriet's graves and to information about Harriet's bequest.

The limitations of this work did not allow me to do justice to the research done on my behalf in Delia Webster's home community of Ferrisburg and Vergennes, Vermont by Karl DeVine of the Historical Society, Lois Noonan of the public library, Tom Kernan of Rokeby Hall, and my special correspondent, Mildred Baker. Nonetheless, I give thanks.

I was consistently amazed by the resources on the open shelves of the University of Kentucky Libraries. For harder to find items, I received assistance from William Marshall, Director of Special Collections and Archives. The staff of the Lexington Public Library was always helpful, especially at the interlibrary loan desk.

I am grateful to the following institutions for permission to print the letters and manuscripts as indicated in my notes: Garrison Family Papers, Sophia Smith Collection, Smith College; J. Winston Coleman, Jr. Kentuckiana Collection, Special Collections, Transylvania University Library; the Trustees of the Boston Public Library; The Houghton Library, Harvard University; John A. Andrew Papers, Massachusetts Historical Society.

Many other librarians and archivists provided guidance and assistance. My heartfelt thanks to them and to all librarians. No keyboard will ever replace you. God bless you.

Glenelg Country School
12793 Folly Quarter Road
Glenelg, Maryland 21737